BIBLE STUDY COMMENTARY

Psalms

Bible Study Commentary

Psalms

J. STAFFORD WRIGHT

130 City Road, London EC1V 2NJ

Fort Washington, Pennsylvania 19034

© 1982 Scripture Union
130 City Road, London EC1V 2NJ

First published 1982

ISBN 0 86201 113 2 (UK)
      0 87508 157 6 (USA)

Phototypeset in Great Britain by
Input Typesetting Ltd., London SW19 8DR.

Printed in Great Britain by
Ebenezer Baylis & Son Limited
The Trinity Press, Worcester, and London.

General Introduction

The worldwide church in the last quarter of the twentieth century faces a number of challenges. In some places the church is growing rapidly and the pressing need is for an adequately trained leadership. Some Christians face persecution and need support and encouragement while others struggle with the inroads of apathy and secularism. We must come to terms, too, with the challenges presented by Marxism, Humanism, a belief that 'science' can conquer all the ills of mankind, and a whole range of Eastern religions and modern sects. If we are to make anything of this confused and confusing world it demands a faith which is solidly biblical.

Individual Christians, too, in their personal lives face a whole range of different needs – emotional, physical, psychological, mental. As we think more and more about our relationships with one another in the body of Christ and as we explore our various ministries in that body, as we discover new dimensions in worship and as we work at what it means to embody Christ in a fallen world we need a solid base. And that base can only come through a relationship with Jesus Christ which is firmly founded on biblical truth.

The Bible, however, is not a magical book. It is not enough to say, 'I believe', and quote a few texts selected at random. We must be prepared to work with the text until our whole outlook is moulded by it. We must be ready to question our existing position and ask the true meaning of the word for us in our situation. All this demands careful study not only of the text but also of its background and of our culture. Above all it demands prayerful and expectant looking to the Spirit of God to bring the word home creatively to our own hearts and lives.

This new series of books has been commissioned in response to the repeated requests for something new to follow on from Bible Characters and Doctrines. It is now over ten years since the first series of Bible Study Books was produced and it is hoped this new series will reflect the changes of the last ten years and bring the Bible text to life for a new generation of readers. The series has three aims:

1. To encourage regular, systematic personal Bible reading. Each volume is divided into sections ideally suited to daily use, and will normally provide material for three months (the exceptions being Psalms and 1 Corinthians-Galatians, four months, and Mark and Ezra-Job, two months). Used in this way the books will cover the entire Bible in five years. The comments aim to give background information and enlarge on the meaning of the text, with special reference to the contemporary relevance. Detailed questions of application are, however, often left to the reader. The questions for further study are designed to aid in this respect.

2. To provide a resource manual for group study. These books do not provide a detailed plan for week by week study. Nor do they present a group leader with a complete set of ready-made questions or activity ideas. They do, however, provide the basic biblical material and, in the questions for further discussion, they give starting points for group discussion.

3. To build into a complete Bible commentary. There is, of course, no shortage of commentaries. Here, however, we have a difference. Rather than look at the text verse by verse the writers examine larger blocks of text, preserving the natural flow of the original thought and observing natural breaks.

Writers have based their comments on the RSV and some have also used the New International Version in some detail. The books can, however, be used with any version.

Introduction

In the Bible God uses several different types of writing to convey his truth. There are narratives (often with commentary), preaching and exhortation (as in the prophets), laws and regulations, the distilled wisdom of Proverbs, philosophical discussion (as in Job and Ecclesiastes), and poetry (as in the Psalms). Poetry has its own ways. Thus Wordsworth wrote, 'Shades of the prison-house begin to close Upon the growing boy', where a prose writer today might put, 'The teenager is confronted by the reality principle'. See also the introduction to Psalm 6.

Not everyone has a feeling for poetry, but those who read the Psalms with a sense of their poetic, as well as their God-breathed, inspiration will have an extra bonus. In these notes we shall look for intelligible meaning, but shall try not to kill the thrill of poetry. It is worth reading the psalms aloud to bring the best out of them.

Although it does not rhyme, Hebrew poetry has a beat and rhythm, which translations indicate as best they can. The second line is generally related to the first, either expanding or contrasting it.

The Psalms are in five books, i.e. 1-41, 42-72, 73-89, 90-106, 107-150. Some were evidently written for use in public worship; others were the outpouring of the heart in verses that could often be adapted for use by congregations. Thus they resemble the contents of our hymn books. A psalm, like our hymns, may take up one angle of truth without saying everything about God and his working.

Many, but not all, are ascribed to David, who was certainly a great poet, as we see from 2 Samuel 1:17-27; 23:1-7; Amos 6:5. A true poet is usually prolific, and it would be surprising if David were not the author of many psalms. Indeed 2 Samuel 22 gives Psalm 18 in its historical setting.

The text followed is Revised Standard Version (RSV), with occasional references to Authorised Version (AV), Revised Version (RV), New English Bible (NEB), Good News Bible (GNB), Jerusalem Bible (JB) and New International Version (NIV). In addition there are occasional references to the Septuagint (LXX) which is the Greek translation made by Jews in Alexandria from 250 BC onwards.

BOOK I (Psalms 1-41)

Almost all of these psalms are ascribed to David. The name of God is usually Jehovah (today often rendered as Yahweh), indicated in the RSV by capitals, LORD. In the notes we have retained 'Jehovah' as more consistent with Christian devotion.

BOOK II (Psalms 42-72)

The collection in Book II differs from Book I in two ways.
a. There is a variety of authorship. This makes for a variety of theme and approach, such as one finds in a modern hymn book. There is still a preponderance of Davidic psalms, but there is one by Solomon, and several by poets from among Temple musicians, sons of Korah and Asaph.
b. In Book I the sacred Name, Yahweh or Jehovah, is used some 270 times, while the general title for God, Elohim, occurs only 15 times. In Book II Yahweh occurs only 15 times, while Elohim is used some 165 times. The compiler may already have shared the later reluctance to pronounce the sacred name in reading or singing.

BOOK III (Psalms 73-89)

The closing words of Book II do not mean that there are no more Davidic psalms to follow, but rather that this concludes the two books that are basically made up of psalms of David. In fact there is only one in Book III, but there are a few in IV and V. The largest contributor in Book III is Asaph, who wrestles with problems of judgement and the puzzle of God's apparent non-interference, as he did in Psalm 50. There are also four psalms by another group of Temple singers, the sons of Korah, whom we have met in Book II.

BOOK IV (Psalms 90-106)

A collection of psalms on various subjects, especially praise. All anonymous except 90 (Moses) and 101, 103 (David).

BOOK V (Psalms 107-150)

We might perhaps describe these psalms as 'lighter' – with two or three exceptions they do not wrestle with problems. Most are anonymous. There is a particularly pleasing set called Songs of Ascents (120-134).

1 Two ways, two ends

As we read this psalm we naturally think of our Lord's description of the broad and narrow ways (Matt. 7:13, 14). The pictures here are simple, and do not need elaborate notes. We notice, however, one theme which will be developed from time to time in the psalms.

The believer is seen as living and growing (3), and this is what concerns the psalmists, whose primary theme is the believer's growth in fellowship with God. Over against the believer are the wicked, who, like dry chaff, are dead and consequently fixed in their ways. (For a similar picture see Jer. 17:5-8.) The wicked are anti-God, and express this by mentally or physically attacking the people of God.

We may be surprised that the psalmists say nothing about winning the wicked for God, but leave them under the judgement of God now and hereafter. Obviously the psalmists do not think that repentance is impossible (7:12), and in fact they themselves have experienced the grace of God leading to repentance and faith. In proclaiming the glory and goodness of God, they are presenting the basis of the Old Testament gospel. In Israel even the wicked kept up formal attendance for worship in the Temple (Isa. 1:10-20), so they would hear these psalms sung.

The wicked in the psalms are those who at the moment are set firmly against God and his ways. When they are mentioned in the psalms they are usually prayed against, as actually hindering the growth of the believer. Even Jesus Christ realistically recognised that there were those who were firmly set against him, and were likely to remain so (Matt. 12:31, 32; 23:33).

The wicked are generally Israelites, who had every opportunity of knowing God and his ways. As far as non-Israelites are concerned, several psalms speak of the conversion of other nations (e.g. 87), and already David had people like Uriah the Hittite (notice the iah [Jehovah] ending to his name) and Ittai of Gath (2 Sam. 15:19) in his army, and doubtless other converts too.

There is one further thought that we may keep in the background. The Christian's enemies are supernatural powers (Eph. 6:12) who are beyond conversion.

THOUGHT: 'Blessed' (1) is not a pious word. It means 'deeply happy'.

2 God's King

When David was a shepherd or an outlaw, the inspiration of his poems came from the countryside (as in Ps. 1): when he was king, it came from the international scene he viewed from his throne.

We must do an equation. Every king was anointed and when he is spoken of as the Lord's anointed the Hebrew word is 'Messiah', the Greek equivalent being 'Christ'. This psalm shows God's anointed king, and David recognised this as an ideal for himself and his successors, although all fell short. Yet one day the perfect and world-ruling anointed one, the Messiah, would come. Thus the first Christians quoted the psalm when they were talking about Jesus Christ (Acts 4:25, 26).

David came to the throne with many enemies threatening him, and God gave him the victory (2 Sam. 8). He knew that God had chosen him as the leader, and that his life was to be a witness for God. This is what he declares pictorially in this psalm.

Obviously the theme goes far beyond the contemporary scene. The king has worldwide authority, which David did not have, and has the power to make or break the nations, which was not true of David. Indeed, the way to God is through submission to the king, and death is the lot of those who reject him.

We have seen one New Testament reference to Jesus Christ. His public designation as the Messianic Son (7) was made at his baptism (Matt. 3:17) and above all at his resurrection (Acts 13:33). Another quotation (Rev. 2:26, 27) emphasises his judgement of the nations (8, 9).

Yet Jesus Christ did not reign in Jerusalem, except with a crown of thorns on the throne of the cross. We conclude either that the psalm will be fulfilled after Christ's return (Rev. 20:9, 10), or that the earthly Jerusalem described here was a kind of shadow of the Jerusalem which is above, where Christ reigns now (Ps. 110; Gal. 4:25, 26). Could both be true?

The old translation 'Kiss the Son' (12) involves the introduction of a later Aramaic word though accepted by NIV. Suggested changes do not alter the call for submission to the Lord.

THOUGHT: 'What think ye of Christ?' (Matt. 22:42)

3;4 Conflict and peace

Opinions differ over the titles assigning a psalm to a particular occasion. Are they part of the inspired text, or are they suggested applications by collectors of the psalms? Hebrew Bibles count them as verse 1, but NEB omits them. We shall treat them as genuine, whether written by David himself or by a compiler who knew the facts.

The heading to Psalm 4 is different, since it is a musical reference for the temple choirs. In both psalms we note the addition of *selah* after certain verses. This probably indicates a musical interlude, but we can treat it as a pause for thought.

Psalm 3 Absalom had many supporters (1; 2 Sam. 15:12), and Shimei's curses (2 Sam. 16:5-8) declared that God had deserted David (2). David had been urged to take the ark with him when he evacuated the city, but he sent it back to where it belonged, to the holy hill where God revealed himself (4; 2 Sam. 15:24, 25).

David's trust in God allowed him to sleep quietly with the battle so near (5, 6; 2 Sam. 17:27-29). He was confident that God would give him the victory (7, 8), although he did not yet know that he would lose Absalom (2 Sam. 18:9-33).

Psalm 4 Commentators generally link this psalm at evening (8) with Psalm 3 at morning (5). But the psalms may be written simply for two choirs to sing antiphonally. One sings the faith of the believer, while the other challenges the unbeliever to take the way to God. So the believer thanks God for his salvation, and looks for his continued help (1, 3). By contrast, God sees the world going on its way with no regard for his glory (2). Then why not in the quiet realise you are a sinner (4), and come to God by his way of sacrifice (5)? Many say they would serve God if it paid (6), but peace and joy are worth more even than the ordinary good things of life (7, 8).

Translators differ over the first words of verse 4. The Hebrew word means literally *tremble*. Hence the meaning here may be either 'tremble with fear before God' (AV, GNB, JB), or 'tremble with anger' (RSV, NEB, NIV). The former fits the interpretation given in these notes, but the latter appears in Ephesians 4:26 in another context concerning the night hours.

THOUGHT: 'More than all in Thee I find.'

5 Lift up your heart

The title suggests that David wrote this for one of the levitical choirs. It follows on well from Psalm 4. David has slept (4:8), and on waking renews his fellowship with God (1-3). He searches his heart in order that he may not start the day treasuring what God hates (4-6).

So much for negatives, for putting away and clearing up. Now for the positive opening up to God (7). The Temple has not yet been built, and David goes to the tent where the ark rests as the mark of God's presence. The sacred things on earth were earthly translations of heavenly realities (Heb. 8:5), and the tent sanctuary was the focus of the heavenly temple (7, Ps. 11:4). When we come to God in prayer, we too enter the holy of holies, the real Temple, by the way opened up through the blood of Jesus Christ shed in sacrifice (Heb. 10:19-22). Like David, we pray to be led in the way God has in mind for us (8). 'Lead us not into temptation, but deliver us from evil.'

Verse 9 is quoted in Romans 3:13 to describe the world without God. As long as rebels continue to reject him, God's end for them is inevitable (10). But is it inevitable for all? Paul in Romans 3 goes on to speak of God's justification, and hence salvation, of sinners and rebels, and David sees the joyful change when other sinners, like himself, find refuge in God (11, 12). Indeed, in his court he had converts like Uriah the Hittite (the -iah represents Jehovah) and Ittai the Gittite (a Philistine from Gath) (2 Sam. 11:3 and 15:19), and doubtless many others.

THOUGHT: 'Have I any pleasure in the death of the wicked, says the Lord God, and not rather that he should turn from his way and live?' (Ezek. 18:23).

6 Deep depression

This psalm is suitably set for the *sheminith*, a heavy sounding string instrument of the order of our cello or double bass.

Anyone who has suffered real depression will say that David's description could hardly be bettered. Others of us may feel embarrassed by the extravagance of his language. As we shall often meet this sort of language in the psalms, we may note here: **1.** This is poetry. When David says his eye wastes away and grows weak (7), he is not needing glasses. **2.** A poem has its source in a poet's feelings, not his intellect. **3.** Oriental peoples, and indeed many others, lay bare their emotions in a way that horrifies some Westerners.

David is ill. He submits himself to God, as we should always do (1-3). Are we ill simply because we are members of the human race, which is prone to germs, bacteria, and injury? Or is the trouble in our soul as well as in our bones (2, 3)?

It is natural to look for life rather than death (4, 5). The Old Testament shows that the state of the dead (Sheol) was a feeble existence, something like hibernation. The resurrection of Jesus Christ changed all this for the believer, who now departs to be with him (Phil. 1:23).

There were those who wanted David to die (8-10). His sons were ready to dispute the succession to the throne (2 Sam. 15:6; 1 Kings 1:5), and each had his supporters. The higher we rise, the more rivals we have who would like to see us fall. If we do not have such enemies, we may face thoughts unworthy of a Christian that seize us in our weak moments.

A dictionary defines depression as 'an emotional attitude . . . involving a feeling of inadequacy and hopelessness, sometimes overwhelming, accompanied by a general lowering of psycho-physical activity' (Drever).

THOUGHT: 'David's life is overshadowed by depression, yet he sees God as the light in the cloud.'

7 Guilty or innocent?

The psalmist calls this psalm a shiggaion, perhaps meaning a poem with a strong rhythmic beat. History does not mention this Cush. The opening verse would suit the time when David was an outlaw, and many events happened during the years when he was on the run from Saul. Since Cush belonged to Saul's tribe of Benjamin, he could have been a spy who tried to induce David's men to hand him over to Saul (1-5, especially 2).

David commits his cause to God (6-8). He had spared Saul when he could have killed him (3, 4; 1 Sam. 24 and 26), yet now he himself could be the victim of treachery. But he knows that God has no time for 'dirty tricks' (7-11), and often catches the crafty schemer with the fate he has planned for others (12-16).

Although David elsewhere confesses himself a sinner, he here maintains his rightness before God (3, 8, 10). If we use the word *rightness* rather than *righteousness*, we may avoid theological prejudice and also the boastfulness of the Pharisee in the Temple (Luke 18: 9-12). There are right patterns of life which we make our aim. David can truly say that his pattern is loyalty to friends and fairness to enemies (3, 4). There are other patterns for us to follow, and we have the right to ask God to bless us in them because they are the way of rightness. On the other hand the man whose pattern defies God's standards has no grounds on which to appeal for deliverance (12-16). Then let us remember the duty we have to offer what is, hopefully, spontaneous thanks and praise (17).

THOUGHT: 'Thy will be done' in me and for me.

8 A psalm of wonder

This psalm could be killed by a commentary. It is best savoured by reciting aloud, preferably out in the country, perhaps under a blue sky, or under a cloudless night sky, like David, gazing at the march of the constellations as he kept the sheep (3).

A few notes are in place:

a Gittith. Gath means winepress and is also the name of a city. Hence Gittith is either a vintage tune or a Philistine musical instrument.

b The variant translations and divisions of 1b and 2 do not change the essential meaning. Note that God is not thought of as sitting in the sky. Anything away from earth is 'up' but God's 'up' is in a different dimension to the 'upness' of (1b). God does not yet rule on earth as he does in heaven as the Lord's Prayer reminds us.

c 2. Jesus quoted this verse when he was talking about the children in the Temple (Matt. 21:16 uses the Septuagint translation but the meaning is unchanged.) A child has a sense of wonder that breaks through to reality.

d 4. 'What is man?' is asked in Job 7:17 and Psalm 144:3, but is answered differently.

e 4-6. Quoted in Hebrews 2:6-8 as so far fulfilled in Christ alone. We remember that he controlled the wild beasts of the wilderness (Mark 1:13), brought the fish into the nets (Luke 5:4-7), and rode an unbroken colt through the excited crowds (Luke 19:30–38). This was only a small part of his domination (1 Cor. 15:27; Eph. 1:22).

f 5. God. The word Jehovah is used only of the one true God. Elohim (the word here) is a plural form and is regularly used of the true God as a plural of majesty. Occasionally it means supernormal beings, and the Septuagint here translates it as angels. So in Hebrews 2:7. Man is lower than God, and is also a step down from the previously created spirit world.

g 5-8. David thrills to the revelation of Genesis 1:26-30.

THOUGHT: 'The world will never starve for want of wonders, but only for want of wonder' (G. K. Chesterton).

Questions for further study and discussion on Psalms 1–8

1. In Psalm 1 what are the differences between believers and unbelievers? What do you find most challenging about this?

2. In Psalm 2, what message is given to the rulers of the world? Who are the most important and dangerous of today's rulers? Pray for these men.

3. In what ways have you experienced God's deliverance (Psalm 3)?

4. What are 'right sacrifices' (4:5)?

5. Psalms 3 and 4 talk of sleeping peacefully. Why was David able to write this? What would you say to someone who came to you for advice about insomnia (compare 16:7 and see notes on Psalm 63)?

6. What are the characteristics of the wicked in Psalm 5? What is David's attitude (a) to them (b) to God (c) to himself?

7. Do you believe tolerance is a Christian virtue? When is it good to be tolerant, and when bad?

8. Someone has described depression as a great black bird sitting on her shoulder. How does David describe his depression in Psalm 6? What does he do about it? How do you cope with your own depressions and those of your family and friends? What good can come out of them?

9. Does Psalm 8 teach that Christians should join a conservation society such as Friends of the Earth? Why? (Compare also Psalm 148.)

10. 'God's in his heaven, – All's right with the world,' sang Browning's Pippa as she started her day. Is this theologically dubious, unrealistic, or a proper song of confidence in God?

9 Thanksgiving for victory

Some commentators regard 9 and 10 as one, since there is an acrostic, admittedly broken, running through the two. An acrostic psalm starts each verse with A, B, C, etc. (JB indicates the Hebrew letters.) Others treat the two separately, as we shall do.

In David's early days Jerusalem was still an open city. It was thus vulnerable to attack, and this psalm celebrates the rout of some enemies. These may well have been the Philistines (2 Sam. 5:17; 8:1). David struck back, and here poetically describes the total defeat of the enemy (5, 6).

The attack was evidently planned to catch David at a time of weakness, when he was 'needy' and 'poor' (18). It was a malicious attempt, perhaps treacherous (15), to destroy the new capital. David turned to the Lord for help (13, 14) and God answered his prayer (9, 10). David sees his deliverance against the background of God's total rule (7, 8, 17, 19, 20).

The musical notes are now obscure. The strange title of the tune, Muth-labben, means 'Death to the son', but it is as useless to speculate on its origin as it would be to guess why the tune to which we sing some hymn has a strange title in our hymn book. Higgaion (16) is translated in the text of 92:3 as 'melody' (RSV, GNB, NIV), 'solemn sound' (AV), 'sounding chords' (NEB), 'rippling' (JB), so we can only say that the choirmaster would have known what sort of *selah* interlude to play here.

For ourselves we can say that when God gives us a task to fulfil we may find we have personal enemies, and we shall certainly have the attacks of temptation.

THOUGHT: 'We rest on thee, our shield and our defender;
　　　　　'Thine is the battle; thine shall be the praise.'

10 Man of the earth

Those who regard Psalms 9 and 10 as one psalm point out that there is no separate title for Psalm 10, and the acrostic continues. But the theme is different: no longer the rout of an attacking army, but one who selfishly defies God's law day by day. In Psalm 10 we are dealing with the typical man of the world, whose values are 'What's in it for me?' and 'I'll get away with anything I can. What's God got to do with it, anyway?'

If there was no God or no responsibility to God, it would certainly be foolish to curb our own self-interest. In fact verses 1-11 represent a logical view of a self-centred life.

As Christians we often feel helpless before 'man who is of the earth' (18). For in addition to our own troubles there are the brutalities we hear of in other parts of the world which make our problems seem insignificant.

We have a double task. We lift the sufferers up to God (17, 18), and when we do so we wonder at the strength that he gives to Christians in their agony (17b). Ultimately we sadly, yet gladly, know that what is not righted here will be righted before all mankind at the judgement, when God's enemies will be put down (16).

Yet we must not opt out of our responsibility to fight for the right where it is in our power to do so. A Christian cannot leave protest and action to others, nor refuse such influence as comes through voting and, for some, accepting a position in local or national politics. Why should society be at the mercy of the unscrupulous (8, 9)? This was a frequent theme of the prophets. They showed up those who were living by the 'grab' values of this psalm, but in doing so they were addressing the king and rulers who could put things right (e.g. Isa. 5:8-23).

THOUGHT: How far does verse 4 give the key to the psalm?

11 Why not run?

Most of the hymns in our hymn books were not written with some contemporary event in view. The authors commonly wrote of some Christian situation, which hymn books classify under appropriate headings, such as Praise, Suffering, Providence, Temptation. Similarly, it is useless to try to find an occasion for each of David's psalms.

We now come to a group of short lyrics centred in the theme of the believer in an ungodly world. This psalm tells of the need to stand firm in the Lord in spite of appearances. Hunters with their spears and arrows are out after birds. They are waiting in the shadow of the trees ready to kill whatever comes within range (2). A sensible bird would escape to the seclusion of the mountains, and this is how the believer is advised by doubting friends (1; see also Ps. 55:6, 7). As frequently in poetry the metaphor is switched, and now the psalmist is warned that his position is helpless because his foundations have gone.

Today the media are only too ready to shoot down the Christian faith, whenever some new theory of the Bible, doctrine, or permissive morality apparently nibbles away at the foundations. Surely we must run, for we cannot still believe!

The question is, in what is our trust? Whom do we believe? It must be God alone. So the psalm indicates that the foundations may seem to be destroyed, but in reality they are not, for God is the foundation (1, 4). If we give way, we are questioning God's judgement (5-7).

Attacks on the Christian foundations have gone on with little variation down the years. Christians have also been attacked in their basic work of teaching, healing and building up of the church. If God has given us this important work of building on his foundation, we may become discouraged because results are few and there is much opposition. On the human level we would run away, but we are on God's level also. It is God who understands, to whom we are responsible.

THOUGHT: Jesus went to the mountain of transfiguration, not to flee as a bird, but to go back to die (Luke 9:31).

12;13 Light through the clouds

Two more lyrics make no secret of the struggles of the believer. We cannot ignore the differences between the Christian and the world, even if we live in a Christianised society.

Psalm 12:1, 2 is echoed by Elijah's cry of depression, 'I only am left' (1 Kings 19:10). God's reply to Elijah was a reminder that there were still seven thousand in Israel who had refused to worship Baal (1 Kings 19:18). In this psalm, sung to the heavy groaning sound of the sheminith (Ps. 6), David, also, comes to see that there are those who groan to the Lord for help (5).

As king he is aware of the lies, flattering and intrigues of the court (2-4; e.g. 2 Sam. 15:3, 4). He sees the rise of clever talkers, who have their own way in argument. Others are continually on the make, especially in grabbing the possessions of the poor by running them into debt (5; Amos 2:6). From the time of David onward the rift between rich and poor widened. The rise of city life inflated the desire for money and property at the expense of the less fortunate (8; Isa. 3:14, 15). A situation with which our own world is familiar.

God is, however, on the side of the underdog. Someone has said epigrammatically that the Bible shows God to be unfair in that he weights the scales on the side of the poor and oppressed (5). The problem of the promises in verses 5 and 6 is when God will do this. Undoubtedly he will do it in the life to come (e.g. Lazarus in Luke 16:25); but David, and we ourselves, have a duty to be God's agents, helping to fulfil his promises here and now.

Psalm 13, one of Calvin's favourites, takes up the question of 'How long?' (1, 2). In the New Testament, as in the Old, this cry is heard repeatedly. The answer is always in terms of faith, which again and again is seen to be justified, but which may have to be content with the answer, 'Wait'. The fact is that on the stage of the world the enemies of the gospel strut around as the powerful 'baddies'. The ordinary man looks for the ultimate triumph of the 'goodies', and what he senses to be correct the Bible declares to be indeed the purpose of God.

We need not go down to death afraid that God is helpless against evil (3, 4). We lift up our eyes to God in heaven, and know that the sun is ready to break through the clouds (5, 6).

THOUGHT: 'Be patient in tribulation, be constant in prayer' (Rom. 12:12).

14 Sense and no sense

This psalm reappears later as Psalm 53. Psalms 11-13 have presented an increasingly gloomy picture, with the enemies of God becoming more threatening till they seem finally to triumph (13:2). Now we see the reality through the eyes of God, the God whom men are foolish enough to treat as non-existent either in their thinking or in their behaviour.

Verses 1-3 are paraphrased of Jew and Gentile alike by Paul in Romans 3:10-12. Theologians use the term original sin to describe the state of everyone born into the world since the fall. All of us are born with a twist in our nature that soon develops into actual sins. These verses describe all of us when we are left to ourselves.

The refusal to consider the claims of God is the root of all sin. We fix our own standards, as Adam and Eve hoped to do when they tried to become 'like God, knowing good and evil' (Gen. 3:5), without any recognition of responsibility towards God – if indeed there is a God!

Note the sequences in the psalm. Rejection of God leads to moral irresponsibility (1). Yet God does not reject, but leaves an opening for the fool to become wise enough to turn to him (2). The psalm begins to make a distinction. There are some who are determined to go their own way (3), and live at the expense of others (4). Yet, as Paul shows in Romans 3, those who start as sinners may find forgiveness and righteousness in and through the Lord Jesus Christ. So, while all are sinners, there is a new generation of those who are born again (5). Once more, in a confused world, David casts us back upon God as our refuge, and the fool's 'No God' becomes 'God our refuge' (6).

The final verse was probably added when the psalm was used in public worship after or during the exile. To us it has a Messianic significance, since deliverance in the deepest sense came from Zion when the Lord died there on the cross (Isa. 59:20).

THOUGHT: 'We were by nature children of wrath, like the rest of mankind. But God ... made us alive together with Christ ...' (Eph. 2:3–5).

15 A sermon on the mount

Psalms 14 and 15 might have been brought together as an utter contrast. Psalm 14 sinks to the depths, while 15 touches the heights. In its own way Psalm 15 may be compared with the Sermon on the Mount with its portrayal of God's ideals. Indeed this is a psalm of the 'holy hill' (1).

Here we may make an observation which we shall notice a number of times. The tent (which was later replaced by Solomon's Temple) and the hill of Zion are earthly realities, but they are also reflections of the temple of heaven and Jerusalem above (Heb. 8:5; 12:22). Sincere worshippers looked through the shadows to the realities. Others, as the prophets indicate again and again, felt they were discharging their duty to God by 'going to church' and offering the prescribed sacrifices (e.g. Isa. 1:12-17). We may easily find ourselves guilty of a similar attitude, at least on occasions.

So when in verse 1 David speaks of people who stay in the tent and dwell on the holy hill, he is not thinking primarily of the priests and Levites, but of those who press through to the enjoyment of the presence of God, seeing the reality through the 'sacramental' signs. George Herbert (seventeenth century), continually saw spiritual realities in earthly things e.g. his hymn, 'Teach me, my God and King, in all things Thee to see'.

In general this psalm needs no notes, except perhaps where verse 5 says 'put out his money at interest'. The AV translates this phrase 'usury' which can be misleading today since usury has come to mean oppressive demands for interest. Deuteronomy 23:19 forbids charging any interest to brother Israelites, but, since the same verses say that interest may be asked from foreigners, it is clear that interest in itself is not wrong. Note the reference to investment at interest in Luke 19:23. GNB catches the perpetual significance of verse 5 with, 'He makes loans without charging interest'. Christian projects are still helped by interest-free loans.

THOUGHT: An opportunity for a check-up.

16 Life now and hereafter

If this Miktam psalm (probably a musical term) stood by itself, we should assume it was David's cry during some serious illness. In fact this may have been the occasion of writing, and David confidently claims healing from the Lord (9, 10). Yet, when verses 8-11 are quoted in Acts 2:25-28, Peter applies them to the resurrection of Jesus Christ, and rejects their application to David (Acts 2:29-32). As happens from time to time in Scripture, the Holy Spirit guides the writer to use words and phrases that later prove to have a fuller significance than the casual reader would guess to be the case.

David knew from God that the Messiah would come from his line, and some of his psalms reflect this knowledge. Peter rightly says that David was given some awareness of the Messiah's sufferings, death, resurrection and ascension (Acts 2:30, 31), as indeed we shall notice elsewhere in the psalms. Hence in verses 9 and 10 he speaks in the name of his Messianic descendant, and declares that death for him is not to be a long wait in Sheol, nor is his body to perish (Acts 2:31). (The word translated 'the Pit' is interpreted by the Jewish Greek Septuagint and Acts 2:31 as 'destruction', NIV has 'decay'.)

One wonders whether David is writing the whole psalm in the name of Jesus Christ, as he does Psalms 22 and 110. The speaker is the embodiment of the character described in Psalm 15. He is wholly devoted to God and his will (2), and is happy in the company of God's people (3).

Verses 5 and 6 rejoice in the allotment of the good life that God has freely given and the cup of blessing placed in his hands at the feast, a cup that continually runs over (see Ps. 23:5). From time to time Jesus withdrew for quiet meditation, but night and day he sought and knew his Father's will (7, 8; John 8:28). When he died, death could not retain him (9, 10), and he was raised to die no more (11).

Even if we give the psalm a Messianic application, we know that David sought the same pattern of life for himself.

THOUGHT: Verses 9-11 sum up eternal life.

Questions for further study and discussion on Psalms 9–16

1. How can we know when God has given us a task to fulfil (see notes on Psalm 9)?

2. What brutalities and injustices are you particularly aware of (compare Psalm 10)? Discuss these and pray about the practical action which you or your group could take. Is there anything God may be calling you to do?

3. On what sort of occasions are we tempted to fly away? What made the psalmist refuse to escape (Psalm 11)?

4. In Psalm 13 David is experiencing 'sorrow . . . all the day'. What is his only hope? It has been said that the happy people in the world are the wicked, the very selfish or the stupid. Do you agree? Do you think that a Christian who is sad is disobeying God? What help does the example and teaching of Jesus give?

5. People have different reasons for not believing in God (compare Psalm 14). Suggest some reasons and perform a role play of a discussion between a group of atheists and a group of Christians. When it is over, discuss the feelings you had during the role play, and what you learned.

6. 'The modern experiment to live without God has failed' (Schumacher). Do you agree? Give some examples.

7. How can we guard against empty formalism and hypocrisy in our worship? (See notes on Psalm 15.)

8. What parallels are there between Psalm 15 and the Sermon on the Mount?

9. Why did David believe in eternal life (Psalm 16)? What further reasons would you give?

17 Innocence

David has searched his own heart, and dares to ask God himself to search him (1-3). We imagine that this comes before the sin with Bathsheba (Ps. 51). His attitude is that of Paul in 1 Corinthians 4:4; 'I am not aware of anything against myself, but I am not thereby acquitted. It is the Lord who judges me'.

It is easy to be content with selective innocence. There are plenty of things of which we are innocent because our dispositions are not inclined to them. For this we can thank God, so long as we try to feel for those who are strongly tempted to do the things that leave us untouched. We may not be so innocent of sins for which we have never even examined ourselves (Ps. 19:12), sins of omission as well as of commission.

David here speaks especially of innocence of speech and lack of violence (3, 4). However much he had to be violent in war, his attitude to Saul in his outlaw days shows him to be basically gentle (1 Sam. 24 and 26). By contrast he encounters the loud-mouthed plots of Saul to kill him (11, 12; 1 Sam. 20:30, 31; 22:7, 8; 23:2-23).

Finally he considers the two ways of living. One is the way of establishing oneself in the world, 'the sort of man whose lot is here and now' (14, JB). The closing lines of verse 14 may be taken as the attitude of people whose ultimate satisfaction is to pile up this world's goods, have plenty to eat and drink, and pass on something substantial to their children when they die. The AV and the RV bring out this sense, and it represents a popular view of immortality, in which the family name survives in one's children and money. There is nothing wrong with providing for our children (2 Cor. 12:14), but it is wrong to bring them up to value only what money can buy.

The contrast for the innocent man is the climax of walking with God (15). Certainly verse 15 is true of waking each morning (3), but the contrast with verse 14 almost certainly demands a reference to the resurrection morning after the shadowy existence of Sheol. For us, since the resurrection of Jesus Christ, the joy will come when we depart to be with Christ (Phil. 1:23), even though the final full satisfaction will come only at the second coming, when we receive our new bodies after Christ's pattern (Phil. 3:20, 21).

THOUGHT: 'Satisfied with . . .': What satisfies us?

18 The poet delivered

As we read this psalm, we must continually tell ourselves that this is poetry. Otherwise we could wonder whether the cherub was seen as an UFO (10), why an earthquake that exposed the seabed was needed to save David from Saul (7, 15), and whether David had the feet of a deer (33).

The psalm occurs again in 2 Samuel 22. There are a few minor differences between the two versions which interest textual scholars. They probably came when the psalm was set to music for temple worship.

The interesting thing about the title is the addition of 'and from the hand of Saul'. It is possible that David wrote half of the psalm, say verses 1-24, during his outlaw days, and then completed it during his reign as king. Certainly verses 1-24 sound more like a very personal deliverance, while the remainder records the triumphs of a king.

It is interesting to pick out all the pictures, metaphors, and similes that David uses here. To begin with, there are eight pictures of God in verses 1 and 2. (Although RSV uses the word 'rock' twice, the Hebrew has two different words.)

The main image (4-16) is of a drowning man, overwhelmed by the waves. As he sinks to the bottom of the sea, he calls to God, and the same God who revealed himself on Sinai in earthquake, thunder, and fire (Exod. 19:16-18), and who swept back the sea to expose the seabed so that his people could be saved from their enemies (Exod. 14:21), now saves David from the waters (16). David claims that his life has not been after the pattern of his enemies (20-24), and perhaps remembers how twice he refused to kill Saul (1 Sam. 24 and 26).

When he became king, David was faced by attempts of neighbouring peoples to dethrone him and scatter Israel. When he drove off their attacks, he naturally followed up his victories to secure his enemies' submission (43, 44). Verse 42 is again poetry to describe an utter rout. David repeatedly declares that it was God who gave him the strength he needed.

The conquest of the nations is finally achieved by their submission to Christ through the gospel. Thus verse 49 is quoted in Romans 15:9 of the gospel message going to the Gentiles to bring them to God. A similar application of Amos 9:11, 12 is made in Acts 15:16, 17, quoting from the Septuagint.

THOUGHT: Most readers of these notes live in security, and their enemies are trivial. Pray for our brothers and sisters in countries where enemies are as savage as David's were.

19 The double revelation

Many of us have been thrilled by Haydn's magnificent 'The heavens are telling'. Many of us also have been lost in wonder at God's incredible handiwork in the world around. Paul holds that there is sufficient indication in nature to convince a seriously minded person that there is a creative mind of 'eternal power and deity' (Rom. 1:20). This is limited realisation, but Paul says it is enough to stop people ascribing the existence of the universe to dead idols (Rom. 1:21-23), or, we might add, to the forces of chance. Knowing this God, and not simply knowing about him, needs the revelation of the written word of God.

So the psalm falls into two clear parts. The witness of creation is witness to El (the Hebrew word for God in verse 1), which is a general title for the divine Being. The witness of the Bible is to the LORD, Jehovah, who has shown himself and the way to him in both Testaments. Paul makes it clear by quoting verse 4 in Romans 10:17, 18 that a proper view of creation prepares the way for the preaching of the gospel.

A Christian can find great enjoyment in nature as the Creator's handiwork, although some find such appreciation harder than others. Some have thought that verses 1-6 are an old pagan hymn to the sun, but this is unlikely, since night is praised as well as day (2), and the sun is set in its course by God himself (4; Gen. 1:16).

The purposes and joys of the law and testimony are recounted in verses 7-11, as they are in Psalm 119. Meanwhile a check-up against God's requirements leaves David hesitant, since there may yet be 'hidden faults' (12) as well as deliberate sins (13) from which he needs to be made clean. In the future he would enjoy victory over them. Finally he prays positively for his speaking and thinking to be after God's pattern (14).

THOUGHT: Immanuel Kant, the German philosopher (1724-1804), said, 'Two things fill the mind with ever-increasing wonder and awe . . . the starry heavens above me and the moral law within me.'

20;21 Trust vindicated

These psalms are usually taken as companions. Psalm 20 hails the king as he goes out on a campaign, and Psalm 21 hails his triumphal return. The only puzzling feature is the reference to the golden crown (21:3), which has led a few commentators to treat Psalm 21 as a coronation psalm. There are two alternative explanations. It may be a general reminder that he is God's crowned king, or the psalm may refer to the campaign against the Ammonite capital, when David brought back the king's golden crown and it was placed on his own head (2 Sam. 12:30).

Psalm 20 is straightforward. David may have composed it himself to be sung at his departure. The people commend him to God as he marches out (1-5), and the king replies with confident trust in God (6-8). This would be sung in the king's name by a second choir, while the first choir rings out a final appeal (9).

Psalm 21 again may be read simply as a highly poetical celebration of the king's victorious return, the emphasis being on the Lord's answer to the king's trust.

There is also the possibility that once again David is carried forward to the days of the Messiah. Indeed the Jewish targum, which gives traditional interpretations of the Scriptures, puts 'King Messiah' in verses 1 and 7. We can read the psalm in this light without doing violence to its original setting. We might compare the psalm to a funnel, through which David speaks the poem of his victory, and from the wide mouth of the funnel comes the tribute to the Messiah. We shall come back several times to this concept. Every king of David's line was intended to show the messianic God-likeness, beginning with Solomon (2 Sam. 7:12-16). Some came nearer than others, although all fell short.

We may be happy to read the first seven verses of Jesus Christ, raised triumphantly from the dead, never to die again (4; Rom. 6:9), but uneasy at the fierce verses 8-12. This is the judgement, described in poetry, the judgement that is consistently spoken of in both Testaments including by Christ himself. This psalm singles out those who refuse God and defy him, and those who, having encountered Christ and his claims, finally reject him. There have been speculations on exactly how God will judge *all* mankind, but we can see that those who would not be happy to have God in this life would not be happy to have him for eternity.

THOUGHT: Compare 21:4 with John 5:26; 11:25, 26.

22 Suffering to the limit

There are two approaches to this psalm. One view supposes that the psalmist is writing of his own sufferings, but unconsciously fore-shadows the sufferings of Jesus. The other view is that David writes of Jesus Christ only. The writer of these notes takes the second interpretation. The Old Testament preparation for the Messiah had to include a means of identifying him through his death before he came to his glory. Hence God inspired the writing of Psalm 22 and Isaiah 53 directly of him.

In general we note that, whereas David and others ask for God's judgement on their persecutors, this psalm contains no prayer for vengeance, just as Jesus prayed, 'Father, forgive them.'

In particular we note the New Testament quotations.

a The opening verse is uttered by Christ on the cross (Matt. 27:46). His tortured mind may have run over the whole psalm, but these opening words, mysterious as they are, clearly speak of the effect of the black weight of the sins of the world when 'for our sake God made him to be sin who knew no sin' (2 Cor. 5:21). Holiness (3) and sin, like oil and water, must separate.

b Verses 4 and 8 are echoed by the priests and others (Matt. 27:43).

c Verse 15 speaks of the 'I thirst' (John 19:28).

d Verse 16 describes crucifixion. The word in the standard Hebrew text means 'like a lion' (margin) which makes nonsense. The Septuagint, which evidently translated a word containing one different letter, has 'they pierced' or 'they dug'. The shroud of Turin, which apparently bears the outlines of someone's crucified body, shows that the nails were driven through the wrists, but the Hebrew word for 'hand' also includes the wrist (e.g. Gen. 24:22; Judg. 15:14, where RSV naturally translates 'hand' as 'arm'.). The quotations about the piercing of Christ in John 19:37 and Revelation 1:7 are taken from Zechariah 12:10, but the fact is here also.

e Verse 18. Division of the garments, one of them by casting dice (John 19:23, 24).

The resurrection appears in terms of living to spread the gospel through the world (22-31). Note the context of the quotation of verse 22 in Hebrews 2:9–12. The same approach is in Isaiah 53:10–12, 'When he makes himself an offering for sin, he shall see his offspring, he shall prolong his days; the will of the Lord shall prosper in his hand.' Admittedly Psalm 22, unlike Isaiah 53, does not actually record the death of the sufferer, but, if it describes Christ's sufferings on the cross, he is crying out as his life ebbs away. There is a hint in verse 29 of the general resurrection.

23 The Shepherd and his sheep

At least three well-known hymns show the popularity of this psalm: 'The King of love my Shepherd is', 'The Lord's my Shepherd', and Addison's transformation of it to the English countryside, 'The Lord my pasture shall prepare'. Even city dwellers, who know little of shepherding, find comfort in the psalm and the hymns that have been drawn from it.

An analysis can spoil the beauty of the words, but a few brief notes may be in place. 'Restores' (3) could refer to being brought back from sin and failure, but NEB, 'He renews life within me', and GNB, 'He gives me new strength', probably express the meaning.

Verse 4 has been a great comfort to many Christians who have known they were dying. The Septuagint also has 'in the midst of the shadow of death'. The single Hebrew word is used several times in the general sense of total darkness, without a direct reference to death, but it certainly includes death in Job 10:21, 22 and 38:17.

The rod (4) is a club for defence against wild animals or human enemies, while the staff is to assist the shepherd in walking and climbing, and to rescue sheep in difficulties.

While some keep the picture of shepherd and sheep in verse 5 (see John 10:9), it is likely that the poet now pictures the guest in the home of the generous host, and this is borne out by the closing sentence.

Verse 6b is commonly interpreted of the life to come, the sequel to the first part of the verse. The Hebrew means literally 'for length of days', and need not refer to eternity beyond this life. But this is one passage which the Christian is free to interpret in the light of the New Testament revelation without doing violence to the Hebrew.

QUESTION: What special aspect of the Shepherd's care do I need today?

24 The Lord comes in

This is another psalm to read aloud, or even chant aloud! It was presumably written to be sung by two choirs when the ark was brought into the city (1 Chron. 15:16-24). If the ark was taken out on campaigns, as 2 Samuel 11:11 implies, the psalm would be used again on its return. Some suggest that the ark was carried round the city in procession once a year, and, if so, this psalm would be sung when it was reinstalled.

The Lord is hailed as Creator and Preserver of the solid earth, which rises out of the oceans (1, 2). He is the Holy One who may be known by the pure in heart (3-6; compare Ps. 15).

He has made Jerusalem the centre of his revelation, and the ark symbolises his presence. The procession escorting the ark sings out a demand for entry into the ancient city, whose history goes back before the time of Abraham (Gen. 14:18). The challenge is thrown back by the choir within the gates: who is it who comes? It is Jehovah, the all-conquering King of glory, the One who has revealed himself in history as the Lord of the heavenly hosts and of Israel's hosts.

The picture is truly magnificent, but we may wonder whether the psalm has any application to ourselves. There is the reminder of what is needed in those who would go into the holy place (3-6). Moreover in one sense we bear the ark, the special presence of the Lord, when we come together for worship (Matt. 18:20).

There is one more application based on the thought of Revelation 3:20. Our hearts have ancient doors that need to be opened continually to the King of glory. At conversion, certainly, but also as we grow older, for we have the sad tendency to slip into a Christianised groove, to which the King of glory forms only a background.

THOUGHT: Open up, that the King of glory may come in!

Questions for further study and discussion on Psalms 17–24

1. How far do you consider Isaiah 53 challenges the outlook of Psalm 17?

2. In Psalm 18 David surveys some spiritual crises in his life. What has he learned? What have been some crisis points in your life? Draw a chart, graph or diagram illustrating these. In small groups discuss your diagrams. What have you learned from this?

3. How far is nature an adequate introduction to God? Would you agree with Kant (see note on Psalm 19)?

4. Prayerfully read Psalm 22. What new light does it cast for you on Christ's suffering?

5. What does 1 Corinthians 2:2 mean in practice (see thought on Psalm 22)?

6. Rewrite Psalm 23 using images relevant to you.

7. With the help of a concordance, look up the New Testament references to Jesus Christ as the Shepherd. What do you find most encouraging about this teaching?

8. 'Our hearts have ancient doors that need to be opened continually to the King of glory' (note on Psalm 24). Would the realised presence of Christ make a difference in your church and home? In what ways?

25 Self-examination

This is one of the acrostic psalms, where each verse begins with a fresh letter of the alphabet in order. As it stands, the acrostic form is broken more than once, but slight alterations in the Hebrew are possible to correct this.

It is often possible to find a link between consecutive psalms. Thus Psalm 24 has given some of the requirements for anyone who wishes to be in fellowship with the Lord. Psalm 25 is a self-examination to see how far David, or anyone else, has met these requirements. He declares his wish to be in a living and victorious relationship with God (1-3). He wants to be led step by step in the right way (4, 5), and prays for forgiveness of past sins, even those of long ago (6, 7). The Lord receives sinners who truly repent, and helps them to walk in his way and experience his loving care for themselves and their families (8-14).

With verse 15 the picture changes from blessings to pressing troubles. The pilgrim path is neither roses nor thistles all the way, but David has the same response to both. He 'lifts up his soul to God' (1) to enjoy his good gifts, and turns to God when he is tangled in the net of troubles (15). (The imagery is taken from trapping; nets are laid to ensnare wild animals.)

The net David is tangled in is loneliness and inner distress (16, 17), and some of his troubles may be due to his own sins (18). Other troubles come from personal enemies (19). The section closes with a restatement of its theme: in God is our refuge, and God looks for integrity. David does not claim perfection, but accepts God's ideal as his, and declares that any fulfilment of the ideal can come only as he waits on God (21).

The final verse was probably added when the psalm was taken for congregational use. What is true for the individual is true for the church as a whole, and for the nation if it is to prosper.

THOUGHT: 'What does the Lord require of you but to do justice, and to love kindness, and to walk humbly with your God?' (Micah 6:8).

26;27 In the presence of God

Psalm 25 took up one aspect of Psalm 24, the requirements of the man of God. These two psalms include this, but go on to consider what 24:3 means by ascending the hill of the Lord and standing in his holy place. We have already seen the inner meaning of this picture in the notes on Psalm 15. David and others loved the worship in the sacred tent and later in the Temple, but they pressed on to experience the heavenly realities.

So in 26:1-5 David once more examines his life, first positively (1-3), then negatively (4-5) – both essential for a true self-examination. Only then does he dare to approach God. The priests had to wash their hands before going to the altar to offer sacrifice (Exod. 30:17-21). David takes up the symbolism, and may well link the washing away of the dirt of sin with the altar of sacrifice for sin (6-8).

Since we are taking the two psalms together, we note the same desire for dwelling in the house of the Lord in 27:4. The worship is in verse 6, but the constant walk in the Lord's presence is seen in verses 7 and 8.

A remarkable book, continually reprinted, *The Practice of the Presence of God*, by the seventeenth-century Brother Lawrence, describes what is evidently David's aim. Some of the readers of these notes will understand this experience, while to others it will seem too mystical. The Bible has a message for the inner-worldly, for the theologically or ecclesiastically precise and for the activist, and there is no ultimate contradiction between them. The body of Christ would be impoverished if one of the three held exclusive possession, but it may well be that more of us would find a fuller satisfaction in spending more time in quiet meditation on the Lord and enjoyment of his presence, without sacrificing sound, revealed theology and active involvement as Christians in the things of daily life.

We note again the attitude to sinners. David knows that the way to fellowship with God is first breaking with sin. Continuing in sin is to renounce fellowship with God. If the former means that we have God's hand upon us, the latter must mean God's disfavour, which, if the sin continues, will bring ultimate judgement. Hence David's underlying thought is, I am on God's side, therefore I am against sin and those involved in it.

THOUGHT: 'Whoso hath felt the Spirit of the Highest
Cannot confound nor doubt him nor deny:
Yea, with one voice, O world, tho' thou deniest,
Stand thou on that side, for on this am I.'
(F. W. H. Myers, *Saint Paul*)

28 The Lord my strength

In the previous psalms David has admitted his sins and has asked to enjoy the sense of God's presence. In this psalm he does not confess any sins directly, but he disentangles himself from the ways of those who have no time for God (5), and who are ready to deceive their neighbours (3). These people have no hope beyond death, but descent into Sheol is the end for them. David, with his link with the living God, knows that, although he will die one day, there is hope beyond the grave, and he is not to be taken off with those who simply die (1, 3; Ps. 49:14, 15).

As we have already seen, he looks beyond the earthly sanctuary to the eternal holy dwelling place of God, and he prays to 'Our Father, who art in heaven' (2). The result is an inner confidence, equivalent to what the New Testament describes as 'hope', the steady attitude that comes from faith (6, 7).

David has been speaking as an individual, but he is also, as God's anointed, the leader of a great people. What he prays for himself, he prays in their name also, and thus adapts the psalm for public use (8, 9). We may be more individualistic than corporately-minded in our approach to God, but the Bible brings both attitudes together.

When David here prays against the workers of evil, he has in mind the overthrow of their schemes in this life (4). He prays that what they plan for others they may experience themselves on the principle of the measure (Matt. 7:2) and of sowing and reaping (Gal. 6:7). If they were to show any signs of a change of heart, David would doubtless welcome them. Meanwhile he takes them as they are.

THOUGHT: We see how the wicked are requited. Are we prepared to be requited ourselves?

29 God of the storm

David is bold enough to enjoy God as the Lord of the storm. Most of us dread the storm, with its damage to property and danger to life (e.g. Ps. 107:25-27). Yet when David had been shepherding the sheep, and had bedded them down in the valley after observing the signs of storm, he must have been struck by the magnificence of its raging. The writer of these notes will never forget standing on an island in a 90 mph gale, and shouting Psalm 150 in words that he could not even hear for the wind!

Some suppose that this psalm has in mind the Canaanite storm god, Hadad-Baal. If so, this is David's answer. It is Jehovah the Creator who is supreme, and not alleged gods or angels, who must all own his Lordship (1, 2). See further note on Psalm 82.

David even calls on the heavenly beings to confess the power of the storm through which God spoke (1, 2). A mighty thunderstorm sweeps in from the sea (3) and roars southward across Lebanon and Hermon in the north (6, Deut. 3:9) down to the Kadesh wilderness in the south (8). Here is the unleashed power of God's created order, as the lightning carves its way through the forests (5-9) and the rain comes down in sheets (3, 10).

The margin of verse 9 shows how a slight change in the Hebrew letters makes the words refer either to the felling of trees (RSV, JB, GNB, NIV) or to the hinds giving birth under the shock of the sudden storm (AV, RV, NEB).

Now the voices of praise are heard in the heavenly temple giving glory to God (9, 10), and the final verse shows that, although the way of the storm may seem blind, the blessing of the Lord is personal.

Storms that bring disaster naturally raise problems, but this one does not. It does not injure anyone, but, as part of God's ordered round of nature, it tears up old trees to make room for new growth, and brings needed rain.

THOUGHT: The quiet and the storm both speak of God to those who have ears to hear and eyes to see.

30 The ups and downs of life

It is difficult to see how this psalm fits the dedication of the Temple, but the RSV translation of the title is only one possibility. AV, RV, and JB show that the Hebrew word may be translated 'the dedication of the house'. Certainly 'house' may be the equivalent of 'temple' (2 Sam. 7:5, 13), but here it may be David's own house (2 Sam. 7:1), and this would make the psalm more meaningful.

Thus David has captured Zion and makes it the capital city. One of his first acts would be to build a palace for himself, although this would be less elaborate than Solomon's house later (1 Kings 7:1). The dedication of this house then became the dedication of himself (v. 12), after a recital of the varied experiences that had brought him to the throne with God's hand upon him. Very few of us remain on the level of the smooth promenade. We have hills and valleys, and the hills need climbing.

David begins with the pit of his outlaw days, when his life was continually threatened by Saul, and God drew him up on to solid ground (1-3). He calls on God's people present to join him in praise (4, 5).

Yet on the mountain top David had begun to boast of his prosperity as though he had achieved it by himself. Immediately clouds came over the sun, and clouds on a mountain bring cold and danger (6, 7). The danger came in an illness which can bring down the king, or the executive, just as it can the ordinary member of the public. His help-lessness turned David to prayer once more (8-10).

God heard him, and brought him to the throne. Now he determines that praise and thanks to God will be an essential part of his life (11, 12).

Thus the atmosphere of the house is irradiated by the dedicated lives of those who live in it, and by those who come in as visitors.

If we are not having a house-warming in the near future, we may take up the meaning of the psalm in the continual dedication of the house of our life, our body being the temple of the Holy Spirit (1 Cor. 6:19). On the heights we give the glory to God, and in the valleys we look up in trust that he will turn the night of depression into the morning of joy (5). This may sound too simple a way to live, and the morning may seem long in coming, but it is the way of dedication.

THOUGHT: 'Like living stones be yourselves built into a spiritual house . . . to offer spiritual sacrifices acceptable to God through Jesus Christ' (1 Pet. 2:5).

31 The valley of loneliness

The puzzling feature of this psalm is the sudden change of mood in verses 9-18, but this is not so different from Psalm 30:6-10, except in the vividness of the language. There are some parallels here with Jeremiah, especially the phrase 'Terror on every side' (13; Jer. 6:25; 20:3, 10; 46:5; 49:29). It has been suggested that Jeremiah himself might be the author of this section, and the description would certainly fit his sufferings. On the other hand, Jeremiah could have picked up the phrase from this psalm of suffering.

It is hard to imagine that these verses applied to David as king, but they could well belong to his outlaw days when he took refuge with Achish of Gath, and barely escaped with his life (1 Sam. 21:10-15). At this time he could have written the cry of anguish of verses 9-18, when the Philistines at the court cold-shouldered him and influenced Achish to drive him out. He could have had some genuine illness in addition to his faked madness.

This period stayed in David's memory, as is shown by the headings of Psalms 34 and 56. Now, when he gives thanks for his deliverance (1-8, 19-24), he remembers how he had spurned the Philistine idols (6), and incorporates the poem that he wrote then, to show how deep had been the valley before God had lifted him to the heights.

A few of the readers of these notes will have touched the lonely depths of verses 9-18. Others have been down only a little way. Yet we know that these are experiences through which many are passing today, in social ostracism, persecution, imprisonment and the threat of death.

PRAYER: 'Remember them, O Lord, as you remembered David.'

32 All of God

The significance of *maskil* is unknown. Thirteen psalms include it in the title, some by other psalmists than David (e.g. 78 and 89), and it occurs in 47:7 (margin). Some translate it as *Contemplative poem* or as *Teaching poem*. Others treat it as yet another musical term.

From time to time one meets someone who loves to tell stories about himself. In all of them he comes out on top, so that one longs to ask him, 'Did you always win? Didn't anyone ever get the better of you?' After reading some of the psalms we might want to ask David the same question. All that he has written is true, but has he overloaded one side? Even a Christian testimony of what the Lord has done may unconsciously convey the impression of the great things we have done in his service.

But there are psalms in which David admitted defeat. Psalm 25 was one, but this one goes deeper. The king whom God brought to the throne was simply a forgiven sinner. Paul in Romans 4:7, 8 quotes verses 1 and 2 as an example of God's free forgiveness without anyone being able to say, 'Look what I've achieved!' We see what is involved from God's side. He forgives, covers, clears from guilt, so that we can walk with our spirit sincerely opened up before him (1, 2). Forgiveness was in anticipation of the atoning death of Jesus Christ (Rom. 3:25, 26). Now, as Christians, we look back on history, and know that our sins were borne away by the Son of God on the cross.

The psalm breathes humility and brokenness. Unconfessed sins dry up the whole personality (3, 4). Honest confession opens up the liberty of verses 1 and 2 (5), and perhaps verses 6 and 7 picture the new deliverance from the great waters of temptation.

David is not the great man who has overcome. He needs the guiding hand of God step by step. This is better than having to be violently jerked back after going his own way (8, 9; 1 Cor. 11:31, 32).

The psalm ends with a new view of the heights. The valley of sin in this psalm replaces the valleys of physical suffering in Psalms 30 and 31. And the experience of the mountain is the joy of God's unearned, steadfast love (10, 11).

THOUGHT: In heaven we shall see even more clearly that 'Salvation is of God' (Rev. 7:10).

Questions for further study and discussion on Psalms 25–32

1. Psalms 25 and 27 talk of waiting for God. What do you think this means? (See also notes on Psalms 26 and 27.)

2. Think of the people who look to you for leadership and help. Pray for their needs.

3. In Psalm 29 what causes David to worship God? What do you find most reminds you of the glory of God?

4. In Psalm 30 David says his trouble came because he was too confident (6, 7). In David's case, what caused this? Are there areas in which your church also suffers from too much confidence? What is the result?

5. How can we guard against over-confidence in ourselves?

6. Why was David feeling so lonely when he wrote Psalm 31? Have there been times when you have been lonely? What was the cause? Was there a cure?

7. Are there groups of people you know who are lonely, or are shunned? What is the reason? Is there anything you or your church could do about this? How can one find out?

8. In what way does lack of prayer favour the success of sin (Psalm 32)?

33 Te Deum

The editors of the psalms have selected one without a title to follow the call to rejoice in 32:11. The sadness of being beaten by sin gives place to the joy of praise to the Lord who has changed sin for righteousness (1-3). The psalm shows God in all his glory. Man experiences him as utterly dependable, utterly good and utterly loving (4, 5).

The phrase in Genesis 1, 'and God said', shows creation by his word. This psalm speaks of the creation of the heavens and the heavenly bodies (6; Gen. 1:14), and the gathering together of the seas so that dry land might appear (7; Gen. 1:9). The poet depicts the Creator's control of the mighty ocean as the bottling up of the waters (in a skin bottle). Some translations follow a slight emendation and read 'as an heap'. Then comes the solid earth for human habitation, and God created men and women as his representatives in the world (8, 9; Gen. 1:26, 28).

Yet man disobeyed, and now there are two ways: there is 'the counsel of the Lord', which is eternally dependable, and 'the counsel of the nations' who are determined to go their own way (10, 11). God's blessing rests on those who choose, or are chosen, to follow the former (12).

None is hidden from God. All are made after the same human pattern (13-15), and yet so many rest their hopes on power rather than on God (16, 17; see also 20:7 and Job 39:19-25). By contrast there are those whose confidence is in the Lord, and who try to serve him in life and under threat of death (18, 19). The psalm ends with a congregational prayer of renewed dedication.

How are we to interpret verse 10 in the light of continued national and international wrongs? The psalmist was as aware of them as we are. He did not look for immediate results, and he knew that God has given individuals and nations a relative freedom. But down the years evil recoils on those who make it their life-style.

THOUGHT: 'Glory to God in the highest, and on earth peace among men with whom he is pleased' (Luke 2:14).

34 Saved to serve

We tentatively connected Psalm 31 with David's time in Gath (1 Sam. 21:10-15), and the title of Psalm 34 makes the same connection, although the king is called Abimelech and not Achish. Abimelech is probably a Philistine royal title like Pharaoh in Egypt. Thus two kings of Gerar, a city colonised by Philistines, bear this name (Gen. 20:2; 26:1). The title probably means 'The king my father'.

This psalm again is in acrostic form, and some hold that David would not have written such an artificial poem after his exciting escape. But, since the acrostic involves no more than beginning each verse with the next letter of the alphabet, it is easy to write a poem of this recognised type.

The first ten verses are the exuberant bubbling over of a man who has escaped death by the skin of his teeth. There are certainly occasions on which we are carried away like David into the happiness of praise. We have indeed tasted and seen that the Lord is good (8).

In verse 11 David addresses his 'sons' (NEB, NIV 'my children'). At this time David had no children of his own, but the story that follows immediately on the Achish incident shows David gathering a number of followers round him at the cave of Adullam (1 Sam. 22:1, 2). He was their father figure, and here he addresses them affectionately as his children, as Jesus addressed his disciples (Mark 10:24; John 21:5). Those who join David have to understand his ideals. We can imagine him sitting in the firelight, telling of his escape, and singing this and other psalms.

He wished all his followers to share what he had come to believe so far. They wanted a long life, but life without moral discipline leads to destruction (11-14). Moral discipline to be effective calls for prayer in daily events (15-18).

The confidence of verses 19 and 20 may seem exaggerated. Certainly the Lord delivers his people, but they may first have afflictions from which they seek deliverance (19). However, by faith the believer knows deliverance will come, and so he is strengthened. A Christian inevitably extends verses 21 and 22 to the judgement after death. We note that 1 Peter 3:9-12 quotes verses 12-16 in a context of continuing suffering.

The work of guardian angels (7) is difficult to fit into our theology, since what can they do for us that God the Holy Spirit does not do? Yet they have a place in God's government of the world (e.g. Heb. 1:14), although they are never to be prayed to or worshipped (Rev. 22:8, 9).

THOUGHT: The hymn 'Through all the changing scenes of life' is an interesting interpretation of this psalm.

35 Lord, vindicate me

A likely period for this psalm is during the months David spent at Saul's court (1 Sam. 18). His success in commanding campaigns (18:13-15) was likely to incur the jealousy of older leaders as well as of Saul himself, and they would take every opportunity to damage him.

This is the first of the 'imprecatory psalms' which we shall meet several times, and, since this psalm does not need any explanatory notes, we may consider the significance of some of these prayers.

a It is right to be right, since this is to be on God's side.

b It is right to ask God to help us to hold our position, provided that we allow him to correct us if we go wrong.

c It is right to ask God to vindicate us, and so to vindicate his own principles.

There is little moral difficulty over vindication. If we are right in God's sight, we want others also to accept his principles. The difficulty begins when prayer for vindication becomes prayer for vengeance. Then we remember Christ's words about turning the other cheek (Matt. 5:39-41).

d We are now thinking of judgement, including final judgement, or retribution. When sin came into the world, God roused in the human mind an instinct for justice that has persisted – sooner or later we feel that the 'baddies' must go down. We are uneasy about books and films that conclude otherwise.

e Since the coming of Jesus Christ we have a clearer view of the future life and future death. We know that one day the world will see retribution or repayment (not revenge). In David's time very little had been revealed about final judgement.

f Hence prayer for the removal, or overthrow, of the 'baddies' is commonly couched in terms of this life.

g David was acting in the spirit of 'Vengeance is mine; I will repay, saith the Lord' (Rom. 12:19). While he suggested a way out, he left everything to God. Thus his statement in verses 13 and 14 shows the attitude with which he spared Saul's life (1 Sam. 24 and 26). He was not vindictive.

The word vengeance, for which the psalmists look to God, has several shades of meaning. 1. Revenge. This suggests the indiscriminate rage of a dictator. 2. Avenge. Suggests compensatory retribution that is legitimate in character and in proportion to the offence. 3. Vindicate. See notes. How do these shades of meaning fit here?

THOUGHT: 'Can you leave your honour in the care of your heavenly Father?' (H. L. Ellison).

36 Earthbound or heavenbound

David sets us a good example here. He takes a realistic look at wickedness (1-4), but, instead of dwelling on it, he outweighs it with the magnificence of God (5-9). Sin is lodged in the heart and forms an inner voice (1; Mark 7:21-23). When one has dismissed God one easily finds oneself involved in trickery (1, 2) by speech, actions and plots, and carrying out one's schemes at any cost (3, 4).

By contrast, David rises to the heights in piling up the glories of God, each one a challenge to the ideas of the wicked (5, 6). Here again we can absorb the poetry. Have we eyes to see 'the mountains of God (*el*)' towering against a blue sky (6)? Less poetically, we can analyse the phrase as 'the lofty mountains' (NEB).

Does all this sound too remote? Then consider God's love shown to those who look to him (7-9). Food and drink (8, 9) take the Christian straight to Christ as the bread of life (John 6:35) and the living water (John 4:14; 7:37).

When time permits, it is worth taking a long meditative drink of the living water, which starts in Eden (Gen 2:10) and flows triumphantly through to Revelation (Rev. 22:1, 2). It bursts out of the rock in the wilderness (Exod. 17:6; Num 20:11; 1 Cor. 10:4) and nourishes in drought (Ps 1:3; Jer. 17:8), unlike the stagnant broken cisterns (Jer. 2:13). It makes us like watered gardens (Isa. 58:11), or alternatively it gladdens city dwellers (Ps. 46:4). As we walk along the bank, it becomes deep enough to swim in (Ezek. 47:5), and wherever it goes it gives life (Ezek. 47:9).

Its ultimate source of livingness is Jesus Christ and the Holy Spirit (John 7:37–39; 19:34), so it is not just a subjective experience. No wonder that the Bible closes with an appeal to us to quench our thirst with the water of life (Rev. 22:17), as free as when Isaiah offered it (Isa. 55:1). But what flows in must flow out (John 7:38).

The psalm ends where it began, with the wicked, only now they are earthbound indeed (12).

THOUGHT: 'If then you have been raised with Christ, seek the things which are above, . . . Set your mind on things that are above, not on things that are on earth' (Col. 3:1, 2).

37 Blueprint for society

On reading this acrostic psalm, one's first impression is, 'This is too good to be true. Things don't always work out like this.' Certainly they don't, and the Bible is well aware of it. But suppose we take this as David's declaration in his old age (25) of what he has tried to bring about under God in his government of the nation? David had his ups and downs, but he tells us in his 'last words' that he has always tried to rule justly over men in the fear of God (2 Sam. 23:3).

So this psalm relates how God's ideal society operates, and consequently how a king and his subjects can work together to make it effective. Thus verse 25 was true in David's reign, and the righteous poor were always taken care of. In later times the law courts were corrupt, as the prophets indicate, but David was sincere in seeing that the innocent were vindicated and the wicked restrained, which is the theme of a number of verses. In verses 32 and 33 David's judges give responsible decisions, unlike the judges in Isaiah 5:23.

Naturally there are always people who manage to escape the law, but they cannot ultimately evade God's judgement (12, 13).

So we are not to treat this psalm as a statement of what happens automatically, as though, for example, the righteous can put their feet up without trying for a job, but waiting for pennies from heaven (25). We, too, are involved in caring for our brethren in need, and we cannot tolerate a state where any person can starve.

We can thank God if we live in a country where good laws are properly administered. But, whatever the situation, we turn to God and co-operate with him to carry out his ideas in our personal lives and in society.

Did Jesus Christ have this psalm in mind when he quoted verse 11 in Matthew 5:5? The same Hebrew word may be translated either 'earth' or 'land'. The beatitudes, also, are blueprints for God's people in a difficult world.

THOUGHT. The qualifications for possession or inheritance (9, 11, 22, 29, 34).

38 Darkness comes over me

This is one of a group of penitential (repenting) psalms, to which we have not called special attention before. It was held by Delitzsch, a great commentator, that Psalms 6, 32, 38, 51, are all a sequel to David's sin with Bathsheba and Uriah, and should be read in that order. This makes good sense.

These notes, however, are treating each psalm separately, and we see that Psalms 6 and 38 are concerned with enemies as well as illness. Possible occasions for any of these psalms, except 51, would be during David's successes under Saul, when undoubtedly he incurred the jealousy of Saul and his supporters (1 Sam. 18); his outlaw period, including his stay with Achish, when the Philistine leaders threatened him (1 Sam. 21:10-15); the period of unrest during his reign (2 Sam. 13-15); his flight when Absalom rebelled (2 Sam. 15-18); and finally his last illness when Adonijah and his supporters seized the throne (1 Kings 1).

We could place Psalm 38 during David's flight from Absalom, when some of the leaders turned against him. At this time we know that David was burdened with a sense of sin, so that he even accepted the curses heaped on him by Shimei, although he looked to God for a possible vindication (2 Sam. 16:5-14). David's vitality also was at a low ebb (2 Sam. 16:14).

The relevance of this psalm to us does not depend on our ability to place it in history. Maybe things have gone wrong for us, and we can trace our troubles to our own sin. One or two may have turned against us, and have taken an unreasonable advantage of our trouble. Our reaction could well have been what today is termed a psychosomatic illness. In so far as we have done wrong, the way out is confession and casting ourselves on God.

We may not in fact be dealing with illness here. Some commentators suggest that David is describing the collapse of his fortunes under the picture of a terrible illness that has fallen upon him. Was he really suffering festering wounds (who inflicted them?), rotting flesh (5, 7), blindness (10), deafness and dumbness (13)? This means that we can apply the psalm at any time when darkness has come down on us, and we are ready to admit responsibility before God.

THOUGHT: The cereal offering was a memorial (Title and Lev. 2:2). Why is this psalm especially appropriate?

39 Please tell me what I am

Today one finds many people who are trying to discover their identity. Who am I, and what is the point of life? In a sense this psalm asks a similar question.

David is careful how he asks. He does not want to raise his problems in front of the wicked (1-3). The wicked in these psalms are not necessarily criminals, but they are the people of the world whose life-style deliberately leaves God out. David may not want them to seize on his difficulties and publicise them – a salutary thought for theologians who write popular books that appear to overthrow basic truths of the Christian faith. The media love it!

Or David may mean that he will not find the solution of his problems from the people who leave God out. Again, so many chew over their doubts with one another without looking to the Bible and the Christian message.

David turns afresh to God for his answer. How short life is! Maybe if we knew what even its brief length will be we could plan within its compass (4, 5). But how would we plan; indeed how do we plan? Often by a frantic attempt to give substance to the shadow by amassing goods that must all be left behind (6; Luke 12:20, 21).

No, the only permanent security is faith in God (7). We admit that we are sinners in a sinful world, and, when some unforeseen setback comes, we examine ourselves to see what God would have us learn from it. David is certainly aware of his sins (8-11). One thing he learns is the wonder that, after all, he is accepted as God's guest, received in his house as he passes along the journey of life. Although he is in one sense a stranger, the law said of the sojourning stranger who comes in, 'You shall love him as yourself' (12; Lev. 19:34).

It seems strange that David should ask the Lord to look away from him (13), but this is in the context of verse 10. Since he is aware that his trouble has followed on from sin, he prays that God will forgive, and no longer 'frown on me' (NEB). Then he will pass the rest of his brief life in glad fellowship with God before he leaves this world.

Note. Jeduthun in the title was a leading singer in the Temple, and also played the trumpet (1 Chron. 16:41, 42). In addition he was the king's seer, having had the gift of prophecy and interpreting God's will to David (2 Chron. 35:15).

THOUGHT: 'The image of God is worth more than all substances, and we give it for colours, for dreams, for shadows' (John Donne).

40 Total obedience

There are two puzzling features about this psalm. The less important is the apparently wrong order of the sections. Verses 1-10 are praise for deliverance, while verses 11-17 are a cry for deliverance. It is possible that there are two psalms here, especially as verses 13-17 are repeated as Psalm 70, but one still asks why a compiler should create a wrong order instead of adding the other psalm at the beginning.

Probably the solution lies in human experience. High water happiness is often followed by low tide depression. The triumph of victory is once again tested, and once again is vindicated. Instead of complaining that God has let him down after all, David once more searches his heart (12), and knows that God will uphold him.

The more important puzzle lies in verses 6-8, which are quoted in Hebrews 10:5-9, and applied to Jesus Christ. Does this mean that David writes the whole psalm in the name of the Messiah as in Psalm 22? The psalm does not read like this, since it seems rather forced to interpret verse 12 of the atonement. The fact is that David is describing the life of perfect obedience that God is looking for, and this life was seen only in Jesus Christ. God never intended sacrifice to be a substitute for obedience (Isa. 1:11-17). The scroll of the Law (especially Deut. 30) shows what God requires, and David found it a delight to obey.

Hebrews quotes the Septuagint, which has an interesting variant. Instead of 'ears thou hast dug for me' (margin), it has 'a body hast thou prepared for me'. No one has suggested a reason which has been readily accepted, but, just as the RSV and others have had to interpret a difficult phrase, so the Septuagint has paraphrased with an expression denoting a body ready for willing obedience and service. Some connect this with Exodus 21:5, 6.

David and the translators were guided more deeply than they knew. Hebrews shows that the body of Jesus Christ was God's vehicle of perfect obedience, and in his offering of his body on the cross, he fulfilled and abolished every animal sacrifice of the law.

The psalm closes with a perfect balance: the rout of those who are happy to see a believer suffering (13-15), and the joy of those whose heart is set on the Lord and his salvation (16, 17).

THOUGHT: 'My power is made perfect in weakness' (2 Cor. 12:9).

41 A Judas

We have had a run of psalms in which David has suffered from illness and from enemies, and we note his reactions. He recognises that he has sinned and he sees his troubles as God's discipline. Some troubles are the result of sin but not all. Yet even when we are not aware of any special sin that would merit the trouble, God would have us learn some lesson. Thus Job was innocent, but learned a great deal about God and himself before he was restored.

In this psalm David implies that he himself has intervened on the side of the defenceless, and believes that similarly the Lord will intervene on his behalf (1-3). Yet there is also the cry for mercy from one who has done wrong (4).

David is surrounded by enemies who are waiting for him to die, and, when one gains access under the pretence of sick visiting, he talks trivialities as he spies out all the harmful, incriminating facts about the sick man (6). When he comes out, he reports that the patient cannot live much longer (7, 8).

Most devoted leaders have a Judas, and it is not surprising to find verse 9 quoted by Jesus in John 13:18. How well he knew the Scriptures! In the notes on Psalm 38 we considered periods in David's life when these penitential psalms may have been written. It is usual to place this one at the time of Absalom's rebellion, when Ahithophel, David's chief counsellor, turned against him (2 Sam. 15:31. See also Ps. 55:12-21).

Verse 10 need not mean that David will put his opponents to death. Their requital will be their disappointment when David is unexpectedly restored. In fact Ahithophel committed suicide, but David certainly did not pray for this to happen (2 Sam. 15:31).

The final verse is a doxology to round off Book I.

THOUGHT: Is there anyone for whom I wish evil?

Questions for further study and discussion on Psalms 33–41

1. How has your concept of the history of David been modified by Book 1 of the Psalter?

2. Why does Psalm 33 urge us to rejoice in the Lord?

3. If you had the fairy tale's three wishes, what would you ask for? Are you really satisfied with God's giving? If not, why not?

4. 'Saved to serve' (notes on Ps. 34). In what way is this a good heading (a) for the Psalm (b) for the book of Acts? Do you think it is or should be true of all Christians?

5. If someone said to you, 'I want to prove the truth of Psalm 34:8, but don't know how,' what would you reply?

6. What is the place of guardian angels in God's government of the world (see notes on Psalm 34)?

7. To what extent should a Christian be concerned either with his own vindication or with that of another Christian (Psalm 35)?

8. What should be the Christian attitude to the deliberately wicked (Psalms 36 and 37)?

9. Discuss the role of illness in the life of the believer (compare Psalms 38 and 39).

10. Compare and contrast Psalms 22 and 40 in their applicability both to David and to Christ.

42;43 Cry of a refugee

These two psalms are clearly one, as is shown by the refrain in 42:5, 11 and 43:5, although 43 could well be sung as a separate unit. The author is one of the sons of Korah. A comparison of Numbers 16:1 with 1 Chronicles 6:22 shows that there was another Korah beside the family that was annihilated in Numbers 16:31-35. His descendants sang in the worship (2 Chron. 20:19), and also acted as gatekeepers of the Temple (1 Chron. 9:19).

Here one of them is a refugee in the north below the peaks of Hermon and a little (Mizar) height (6), for some reason prevented from returning to lead the Temple worship (4), while his neighbours assure him that God has deserted him (3, 10, 43:1, 2).

He hears the thunder of the cataracts pouring from the mountains, as though they would sweep him away (7), and he longs for the still, refreshing waters of God's presence (42:1, 2). Yet he still puts his confidence in God (5, 8, 11; 43:1, 5) to bring him back to the Temple (43:3, 4). God's light and truth (3) are personified as heavenly guides who will lead him from the spiritual darkness and error that surround him (e.g. 42:3, 10). As Christians we are drawn to Jesus Christ who is the light (John 8:12; 9:5) and the truth (John 14:6).

Throughout the world this psalm will be literally true for persecuted Christians. For most of us it is topical when illness keeps us at home, but it has a beauty for all seasons.

THOUGHT: 'Thou hast made us for thyself and our hearts are restless until they find rest in thee' (St. Augustine).

44 Why should it happen to me?

The psalms involve us in every situation that we are likely to meet. We have already read of thanksgivings for deliverance, but in Psalms 42 and 43 and now here we have believers who seem to have passed beyond God's care. In Psalms 42 and 43 the psalmist placed his confidence in the living God, while in Psalm 44 he turns to the God of history. Both attitudes are correct. Faith in the living God is effective because Christ's death and resurrection are facts of history.

In Book I David often admitted his sin, but here the psalmist has searched his life and declares his comparative innocence. He knows of nothing so bad as to deserve the tragic disasters that have come upon the nation (17-22). Once God had blessed the people beyond their deserts and beyond their own capacity (1-3). Now there is defeat and captivity, coupled with the taunt, with which we too are familiar, 'If there is a God, why does he allow this to happen to you?' (12-16).

How far can we claim to be innocent (17-20)? It is true, as David saw, that, even when we are not aware of actual sins, there may still be hidden sins (Psalm 19:12). Yet we ought to be able to say that we are going forward with constant trust in God. Although we do not claim salvation on this account, we behave as children of the covenant (17), and the New Testament epistles assume that this is possible and indeed desirable. In other words, we are not to be depressed all the time as miserable sinners.

It is important to note that Paul quotes verse 22 in Romans 8:36. Christians today pass through similar ordeals to those of the psalmist. Our own troubles may seem small compared with the physical sufferings of Christians in some countries, but they are nonetheless real.

We read the Bible stories, and see that God is not dead, as our present circumstances sometimes seem to suggest. So we are right to look to him again now. Paul reminds us that, although present history may be against us, it cannot separate us from the love of Christ (Rom. 8:35-39).

THOUGHT: God does not blame us when we tell him of the difficulties that we find in his government of our lives.

45 Hymn for a Royal Wedding

Some have interpreted this psalm, and also the Song of Solomon, as a deliberate allegory of God and the believer, or God and his covenanted people. There is no reason why this psalm should not have been written for a royal wedding; yet, inasmuch as marriage is symbolic of spiritual relationship, the psalm clearly contains elements from which we can gather spiritual lessons (e.g. Hosea 2:19, 20; Eph. 5:21-33; Rev. 21:9).

Nobody knows for which king and queen this wedding song was written. Traditionally it was for Solomon's first marriage to an Egyptian princess (1 Kings 3:1). A tempting suggestion is the marriage of Ahab and Jezebel (1 Kings 16:31), because of the reference to Tyre (12) and the ivory palaces (8; 1 Kings 22:39), but in view of their record as promoters of Baal, it is hardly likely that their wedding song would have found its way into the Jewish hymn book.

The king is hailed for his splendour (2) and his concern to defend the right (3-5). More than that, he is one with God in executing the purposes of his kingdom (6, 7). While this was fulfilled absolutely only by the Lord Jesus Christ, it is possible, as the RSV margin shows, that the text of verse 6 goes even further, and hails the king as God (elohim, so NIV). The quotation of these verses in Hebrews 1:8, 9, with the application to Christ, is open to a similar ambiguity, 'Thy throne, O God' or 'God is thy throne'. Since the verse in Hebrews is intended to contrast Christ with the angels, there is a balance in favour of the former translation.

We realise, as we have seen in previous notes, that often, in speaking of the contemporary king of David's line, the psalmists describe God's ideal for him, although in fact he falls short of it. Yet one day that ideal and perfect Messianic king of the line of David must come. Hence we apply the ideal for the contemporary king to the Lord Jesus Christ.

Having said this, we can see that the psalmist was guided in his choice of expression in verse 6. He and his hearers, knowing that the king was not God, would have interpreted it as 'your throne is God (divine)', whereas God intended the deeper meaning to be realised in due course.

THOUGHT: Consider verse 10 in the light of marriage (Gen. 2:24) and in the light of our inclusion in the church, the bride of Christ (Eph. 5:31, 32).

46 Storm and quiet

This psalm was most probably written after the deliverance of Jerusalem from the forces of Sennacherib (Isa. 37:33-37). God's victory is celebrated in earth-shaking terms, in tidal wave imagery. This is how the enemy have experienced God.

In contrast to the hurricane-whipped seas of verse 3, God's people have found him to be a quiet flowing stream (4). The language is highly poetical, since there is no real river at Jerusalem. This river of poetry flows again in Isaiah 33:21, which almost certainly belongs to this time of deliverance. It is worth using this theme of water for quiet meditation, and in the notes on Psalm 36 there are a few suggestions for texts to use.

The opening words of the psalm attracted Luther in his hymn translated as 'A safe stronghold our God is still', or 'A mighty stronghold is our God', although he paraphrased ideas of deliverance rather than the psalm itself. The psalm may catch hold of our imaginations and feelings, and lead us to recite, or shout, it aloud; its poetry is not limited to any specific occasion, and the words of high triumph may release our spirits.

In verses 8, 9 we join with the poet in longing for the final end of all war and the universal peace that must come, either at the end of the age, or in the millennium, or certainly in eternity (Isa. 2:3, 4; 11:6–9). At present, even though there are more working for peace in the world than ever there were, the cauldron of war is always on the boil, ready to spill over somewhere.

Most of us take the first line of verse 10 as a favourite text, whether or not we practise it. Other translations expand the latent meaning. Thus we have 'pause awhile' (JB), 'let be then (NEB), and 'stop fighting' (GNB). The main thing is that we have a quiet time of prayer, reading, and meditation, a quiet attitude, and an openness for God to work.
Note. Alamoth in the title may refer to a treble voice or to some stringed instrument.

THOUGHT: Picture God's action as fierce torrents or still streams.

47;48 God all-victorious

Psalm 48 evidently belongs to the same deliverance from Sennacherib's army as Psalm 46, and it reads as though the same author wrote it. God's holy city has once more been saved from destruction and the psalmist tells us to walk round the city and see for ourselves that all the walls and towers are intact (48:12, 13). The invading hosts, in which the Assyrians enlisted various petty kings (48:4), have been shattered, as was the armada of Spain. ('Ships of Tarshish' came to mean large ocean-going vessels [7]). This demonstrates God's greatness and love, so there is the same call for quiet meditation as in 46:10 (48:9), reminding us also of the Korahite longing in Psalm 43:3, 4.

Since Psalm 47 comes between these two psalms of deliverance we may assume that *it also* belongs to the same occasion, only this time the author reminds us that it was God himself who originally chose the land and the city to be the glory of himself and his people (47:4).

As one reads about this victory one cannot help thinking of the supreme victory of God in the cross and resurrection, followed by Christ's 'going up' (47:5) after the triumphant completion of his work, to sit on the throne which is the centre of all power in the universe (47:8). One need not worry too much about God going 'up'. Any centre or sphere that is away from the earth is 'up' in relation to any point on earth. Our children must hear of what God has done already in history in providing the gospel of redemption and deliverance (48:13); and also of what he will be to us all through our life because he is the living God (48:14).

THOUGHT: What heritage has God chosen for us (47:4)?

49 A tract on death

This is an unusual psalm, since it is a tract addressed to anyone in the world who is ready to do some serious thinking (1-4). Its arguments are unanswerable.

a People accumulate money as though this will enable them to cheat death, to bribe God, as it were, to give them everlasting existence (5-9).

b Sheer observation shows that no one is clever enough, or silly enough, to escape death, and everything has to be left behind (10).

c Their bodies, that meant so much, now lie in the little plot of earth which is all that is left to them after the rich lands that once they owned. If you enquire for Mr. X, you are shown Villa X, named by the locals after him (11). It was a common idea in the ancient world that one's only immortality lay in the continuance of one's name in lands and descendants.

d In other words, they are simply on a level with the animals, who live for the passing moment and then die (12).

e For such people the bad shepherd, death, guides them to the land of darkness (13, 14).

f There is an alternative. What money and cleverness cannot do, God can. I shall die, but I go into death as a soul redeemed by God and received as his (15).

g 'How much did he leave?' 'Everything'. The sad thing is his wrong estimation of happiness. Without God, men and women are no better than animals (16-20).

Thus the psalm is a marvellous appeal to commonsense. There is no answer to life and death except God, who is greater than both. Having observed the second fact, why not accept the first and trust God? Yet we are still enticed by the second line of verse 18, and in the past, the present, and the future we carry on in the spirit of the slogan, 'What's in it for me?'

Note. Modern translations commonly reject the AV and RV of verse 11, although, if it were correct, it would carry on the thought of the psalm: 'Their inward thought is that their houses shall continue for ever.'

THOUGHT: 'That proverb, A bird in the hand is worth two in the bush, is of more authority with them than are all the divine testimonies of the good of the world to come.' (Bunyan. *Pilgrim's Progress*.)

50 Judgement for saints and sinners

There are twelve Asaph psalms, eleven of them forming the group 73-83. They generally include a theme of judgement. The original Asaph was a singer appointed by David and by Solomon to lead the worship (1 Chron. 6:39; 15:17; 25:1, 2; 2 Chron. 5:12). The Chronicler, as a priest, had access to the Temple records, which were not available to the historians who compiled Samuel and Kings. Some suppose that this psalm comes from an Asaph collection, but was not written by Asaph himself.

It follows beautifully on from Psalm 49. After the warning and appeal comes the sitting of God for judgement. We are summoned to court in the earthly or heavenly Zion, where the judge sits in all his dignity (1, 2). The court officials are fire and storm, and heaven and earth are ready to be called as witnesses (4). There is a similar picture in Isaiah 1:2. The prisoners come up for trial; some will be found innocent, others guilty (5, 16).

First the judge addresses Israel, with whom he has made a covenant sealed by sacrifice (4, 5; Exod. 24:7, 8. Note also Matt. 26:27, 28). The test of obedience is not the multiplicity of sacrifices (8-11), especially if these are treated as bribes to God, as though they could appease his hunger (12, 13). The heart of true sacrifice is thanksgiving and obedience, coupled with prayerful dependence on God (14, 15).

If God's chosen people need to have their priorities adjusted, how much more the type of person who is rebuked in Psalm 49. Whatever lip service he may give to the covenant (16), he has no intention of taking God seriously (17). This means that he lives a purely sensual life (18-20).

The fact that nothing happens to him by way of punishment encourages him to assert that God does not care or even that God agrees with him (21).

This life is not the end. If Psalm 49 spoke of the long darkness of oblivion, this psalm takes us to the judgement beyond the grave (22). If as Christians our conscience does not allow us to thank God for what we are doing, then we are out of God's will, and neither church-going nor any sacrifice or self-denial will put us right (23).

THOUGHT: Christians have their own warning. 'Are we to sin because we are not under the law but under grace? By no means!' (Rom. 6:15)

Questions for further study and discussion on Psalms 42–50

1. The Korahite love of the sanctuary has its parallels in Christianity. Discuss the reasons for this, the benefits and dangers. Do you consider it justifiable?

2. Do you think your church should be kept open all the time? What are the problems? Can they be overcome?

3. Has God given you problems or defeats, which are causing you great difficulty? In this situation what did David (a) do, (b) think about, to help him (Psalm 44)? Are there any other positive steps you can take?

4. Do you think that the longing for the experience of 46:10 is one of the causes of the interest in meditation? What are the dangers of Transcendental Meditation? What is your experience and view of Christian meditation?

5. In Psalm 47, why is the Psalmist so full of praise? Spend some time praying for missionaries you know. What are their particular needs?

6. How would a greater knowledge of church history help us to be more understanding Christians (e.g. knowledge of ways in which early heresies were dealt with)? Is there anything you or your group could do to rectify any gaps you may have?

7. What does Psalm 49 say about death? What are the attitudes to death of people you meet? If someone said to you, 'I never think of death, it's morbid and a waste of time,' what would you say?

8. Rephrase Psalm 50:7-15 to make it apply to your own church.

51 'And can it be . . . .?'

Even if we did not have the title, we should have assumed that this was David's confession after his adultery with Bathsheba and the virtual murder of her husband, Uriah. Although it is easy to spoil the heart cry of the psalm by commentary from the head, it is helpful to trace the sequence of David's confession.

Sin is a stain that only God can obliterate. It needs more than the 'I forgive you', with which one person pardons another (1, 2). Sin is more than doing wrong; it is ultimately against God, however much it involves our fellow human beings (3, 4; Rom. 3:4). Original sin, a twist in our nature from birth and even from conception, is not claimed as an excuse, but it makes us realise our entire sinfulness through and through (5).

Only God can give the inner cure (6), and bring the cleansing that was signified in the law, e.g. the sprinkling with the marjoram type flower heads of hyssop (7; see Lev. 14:4-7 for a leper; Num. 19:6, 18 for impurity N. B. Heb. 9:13, 14). The result is more than ritual cleansing; it is washing whiter than white (7; Isa. 1:18). Then my life, no longer crippled by guilt, will leap for joy in the sunshine of God's presence (8, 9).

The gospel always involves both cleansing from sin and also new life given by the Holy Spirit, whose convicting influence may be killed (Eph. 4:30; 1 Thes. 5:19). Both the negative and the positive bring salvation (10-12). Moreover, a saved person should be a witnessing person (13).

One great sin remains to be confessed and taken away – the contrived murder of Uriah the Hittite (14; 2 Sam. 11:15; 12:9). Yet how could David praise God for forgiveness for this? The law provided no sacrifices to atone for murder (15, 16), and David had sinned 'with a high hand' deliberately (Num. 15:30, 31). He can do no more than cast himself on the mercy of God (in unknowing anticipation of the sacrifice of Jesus Christ?) with a contrite heart (17).

Sometimes this personal psalm was sung in public worship as an act of contrition. The two final verses were added when Jerusalem and her people were ruined through sin. The worshippers cannot bribe God with sacrifices, but, when God restores them, they will bring him the offerings once more. An example of this sort of situation would be that described by Ezra 3:1-7.

THOUGHT: Sin is never single. It has many arms like the octopus.

52;53 'What's in it for me?'

The condemnation of Doeg is worded very strongly in Psalm 52. Could a simple shepherd deserve such a rebuke? But Doeg the Edomite was more than keeper of a few sheep. He was Saul's chief herdsman (1 Sam. 21:7), and doubtless was responsible for a number of under-shepherds and their flocks. Verse 7 speaks of his riches, and he is likely to have been reasonably well off, but David is here thinking of the high reward that Saul would have given him. This would have been for his information (implied in 1 Sam. 22:7) and especially for doing what Saul's bodyguard refused to do – massacring the priests whom Saul held responsible for concealing David (1 Sam. 22:17, 18). Doeg was a foreigner, but he had obviously adopted the faith of Israel, for he worshipped in the shrine at Nob (1 Sam. 21:7). He was crafty enough to suppose that he could destroy David by telling Saul where he could be found (1-4). Sooner or later his dirty tricks will rebound on his own head (5) and the righteous will rejoice at God's vindication (6, 7).

As Christians we hesitate to laugh at a man in his fall (6), but David is using the word 'laugh' in the condensed language of poetry. When God seems indifferent to moral issues, we are bewildered. When the bad man at last receives what he deserves, we are glad that God's moral principles have been justified. At the same time we should be awed, since, 'There but for the grace of God go I'. So in verse 6 we have both the awe and the joy. For the 'laughter' over the redressing of wrongs, see also Psalms 2:4; 37:13; 59:8.

David, unlike the wicked man, looked to God for protection and security. God had delivered and would deliver, in spite of Doeg and others like him (8, 9; also title of Ps. 54).

Psalm 53 follows appropriately, and shows that the two were sung without thought of Doeg in particular, but with the wicked world in mind. Psalm 53 is virtually identical with Psalm 14, except that Elohim takes the place of Yahweh, and verse 5 is different. The same hymns in our different hymn books vary from one another in minor wording, and the variations may be due to the original author. Moreover these hymn books may include or exclude certain verses. e.g. 'He who would valiant be' and 'At the name of Jesus'.

THOUGHT: 'Every man has his price' (Sir Robert Walpole), i.e. will ultimately do something wrong for reward. What was Doeg's yielding point? Where are our dangerously weak points?

54;55 Betrayed

These are two psalms of betrayal. We know the treachery of 54, but can only guess at the Judas of 55:12-14, 20, 21. The story of the Ziphites is in 1 Samuel 23:15–24. They must have welcomed David, but secretly plotted to hand him over to Saul (1 Sam. 23:14, 19, 20). David says of these treacherous men that 'they do not set God before them' (3), for breaking an agreement is regarded as a serious sin (Ps. 15:4; Josh. 9:15, 19). Unfortunately today, both internationally and individually, keeping one's word is of little account, and people think it has nothing to do with God.

The traitor of Psalm 55 is generally thought to be Ahithophel, who went over to Absalom in the rebellion against David (2 Sam. 15:31). He is likely also to be the Judas of Psalm 41. As the wise counsellor he would continually have had close personal sessions with David, and such was his respect for Ahithophel that David speaks of him as 'my equal' (13; NIV 'a man like myself').

David is writing to calm his mind when he is on the verge of the revolution. Ahithophel had already indicated that he would throw in his lot with Absalom, and, as always happens on the eve of a political revolution, there was looting and unrest running through the city (9-11).

David carried out his wish to fly away (55:6, 7), and left the city to be occupied by Absalom. For once he was thoroughly discouraged (2 Sam. 16:10). He was more distressed at the treachery of his friend (12-14) than he was at handing over to his son. He was already growing old, and in old age friendship and companionship are generally worth more than position.

As always, David commits his cause to God (2 Sam. 15:25), and prays for victory in the coming battle (15-19). The prayer in verse 15 is expressive and violent, but it is realistic. When we pray for victory in what we honestly believe to be a justifiable war, we generally shut our minds to the tragedy and death it will involve. Our version of verse 15 would simply be, 'O God, give us the victory'.

Although this psalm is not quoted of Judas, we inevitably think of him. The fact is that any man in a position of influence attracts a Judas to unseat him. Human nature can be very mean.

THOUGHT: 'Friendship is the inexpressible comfort of feeling safe with a person' (George Eliot). Thank God for a loyal friend. What sort of a friend am I?

56 Under arrest

Since there is a similarity between the situations in this group of psalms, we can take the opportunity of picturing how David came to write them. He was clearly a very skilful player and composer on the *kinnor* (1 Sam. 16:16-23). Almost all versions render this as 'harp', although the RSV prefers 'lyre'. It was easily portable.

We may picture a young man today turning an idea into song to the strings of a guitar. David played his small harp in his quiet times before God, sometimes sitting at the mouth of a cave, sometimes by the camp fire, sometimes in his room waiting for enemies to burst in, and then later in his private quarters in the palace. As he went quietly over the words and music, the phrases became fixed in his memory, and at last the prayer was finished and remembered. Often the words were a cry to God, and prayer and music combined to give him peace, as they had given peace to Saul (1 Sam. 16:23).

In the title we have the occasion for Psalm 56 and an attractively named tune. The occasion was David's first stay in Gath, when Achish might have sheltered him, but the Philistine leaders wanted to arrest him (1 Sam. 21:10-15). The heading and contents suggest that this psalm was written before Psalm 34. In Psalm 56 he appears to be under house arrest, whereas in Psalm 34 he has escaped. One must assume that 56:12, 13 were added later as a cry of gratitude to God for his escape.

We have generally tried to apply these psalms to ourselves, since David wrote them about himself as an individual. But there are many other sufferers whom we remember. In the secular and Christian papers today there are accounts of suffering, physical or mental injury, persecution, starvation. Can we pray for these sufferers and try to step out from our needs to feel with them?

Note Verse 8: the sequence of pictured thought is (*a*) God is aware of my batterings. (*b*) My tears of suffering are precious to him. He will save them just as the traveller in the desert saves each precious drop of water in his wineskin. (*c*) God is not simply aware of me, but he has recorded everything about me (Mal. 3:16).

THOUGHT: 'I am thinking tonight, Lord, of all the isolated ones: of all those who are alone, utterly alone . . . Because they have never given themselves to you, Lord . . . Those who have, locked in the terrifying silence of their hearts, a harvest of humiliations, despairs, hatreds.' (M Quoist).

57 Below and above

This psalm belongs to the period of 1 Samuel 22, when David took refuge for some months in the cave of Adullam. He was in constant danger of betrayal and at any time might have been hunted down by Saul and his men.

Some poets may be stimulated to write by some occasion but mostly they are moved by some intuitive idea. The latter is true of nearly all of our hymns, although it is interesting to discover whether any of them can be associated with some event, e.g. *Onward, Christian soldiers* is said to have been written overnight for a children's procession. Although in the present group of psalms David is stimulated to write by some event, we have seen in Book I that he also produces psalms that arise from ideas.

In this psalm we again have the typical sequence of Down – Look up to God – Delivered. We may not undergo the same extremes as David, but in miniature almost every day we have similar periods of Down – Look up to God – Delivered. We note the swing from earth to heaven in verses 4-6. Saul's men are as bad as the lions that roamed Palestine (4; 1 Sam. 17:34). Whereas lions tear with their teeth and open mouths, they are ready with spears and arrows. Yet they are earthbound, while David's God is in heaven (5). Now they are like trappers, but again and again they have been caught out. Thus twice they have incurred their master's wrath through failing to keep David from being in a position to kill him (6; 1 Sam. 24 and 26).

Meanwhile David takes deliverance by faith, and turns his morning prayer into happy song (8). He knows that he is not the only one for whom God cares, so he will tell other nations of God's love and faithfulness (9, 10). Indeed David has done this in his psalms. For Jehovah is the almighty God, and one day all will hail him as the Lord of heaven and earth (11; Phil. 2:10, 11).

THOUGHT: 'Singing and making melody to the Lord with all your heart, always and for everything giving thanks in the name of our Lord Jesus Christ to God the Father' (Eph. 5:19, 20).

58 Called to account

Commentators differ over who is addressed in this psalm (1). All modern translations show in the text and margin that the alternatives are either *gods* or *mighty lords* (NEB, GNB, NIV *rulers*). The Hebrew is *elim*, the plural of *el*, which is normally translated as *god*, but it is thought that both this word and *elohim* could be used of earthly rulers as the representatives of God. The writer of these notes believes that this is unproved, and prefers the translation *gods* here, as also in 82:1.

First we take the usual interpretation of earthly rulers, who are called to account for failing to deal properly with the wrongdoer. It is a sad day in our own times when those who should be preventing crime are found guilty of taking bribes to overlook what is going on in the underworld. When a criminal is found guilty, there is quite rightly an outcry if the sentence is too lenient.

We cannot tell when David wrote this psalm, but presumably it was after he had come to the throne. Throughout his kingdom the towns and cities had their own judges, and evidently some particularly bad judgements had come to his ears. He addresses this psalm to those responsible.

The second half of the psalm is a poet's appeal to God to do what these rulers refused to do and to root out evil from the national life. The cauldron of wickedness will boil over unless God's whirlwind sweeps the fuel away (9).

The poetry in verses 10 and 11 pictures in strong victory words the joy of the righteous when God vindicates his honour. Every time some part of our country's life is cleaned up, the Christian is delighted to see that God's standards are vindicated (avenged).

The other interpretation involves the gods of the nations. Israel was governed by the one righteous God. Other nations, e.g. the Canaanites, believed in immoral and brutal gods and goddesses, and consequently were immoral and brutal themselves. Missionaries testify to real personal powers of evil behind the gods of the people among whom they work, and Paul speaks of these powers as demons (1 Cor. 10:20).

God, or David, attacks these gods and their degrading influence (3-5). Indeed it may perhaps be these deities whose destruction is described in verses 6-9. Then the believers will rejoice to find Satan crushed under their feet (Rom. 16:20), which is one New Testament equivalent of washing the feet in the blood of the wicked.

The essential truth of the need to overthrow evil is present in either interpretation.

THOUGHT: Do we work for what is right (1) in our family, our social circle, our place of work?

59 Waiting to pounce

The heading refers to the occasion of 1 Samuel 19:11, but the words of the psalm suggest that this was not the first time that Saul had sent men to murder David when he left his house, for he had hated David for a long time (1 Sam. 18:29). Indeed it would have driven his wife to desperation if David on the final critical night had sat down to compose poetry instead of escaping! During the 'siege' observers or visitors would report on suspicious characters loitering outside, especially when evening came (6, 14). David's description suggests that they were Saul's 'heavy brigade', not just ordinary servants.

It looks as though verses 5, 8b, 11 and perhaps 13 were inserted for liturgical use, so that the psalm could apply to the nation under stress. These could have been composed by David after he came to the throne. If we by-pass them, we can see David's feelings as the siege continued. He could only leave easily if Saul gave him safe conduct to come and play for him. Even then he was not safe from Saul's violence (1 Sam. 19:9, 10).

Savage, doglike assassins, hostile nations, are always waiting their opportunity to attack. They are God's enemies (8), as are all who treacherously plot evil, such as those who plant bombs to destroy innocent men, women, and children.

Their final overthrow could come in two ways. They may be caught, and their power be checked by a punishment that makes them living warnings (11, 12). Then of course they may repent, as some have in prison, where they have been truly converted. The other possibility is the death penalty, although once again the word *consume* (13) could allow a period for repentance before the sentence is carried out. The result of either action is the vindication of the righteousness of God (13).

Saul's men lost David on this occasion (1 Sam. 19:12), but they were evidently glad to have a further chance to hunt the outlaw and presumably get a reward. Once again David chastised them in his poetry (Psalm 57).

THOUGHT: Some troubles go once and for all, but we may have to bear those that come snarling back again.

Questions for further study and discussion on Psalms 51–59

1. What does Psalm 51 teach about confession and forgiveness? What does the New Testament add to this?

2. Discuss the contrast between the man who trusts in riches and the man who trusts in God. What is the source of your life? How can you be sure you are not deceiving yourself? Discuss ways of checking the truth of your assertion.

3. Why should breaking one's word be a serious sin (see notes on Psalm 54 and compare James 5:12)? If everyone did what they said, how would this affect our national life? How would it affect our individual lives?

4. Why do we so often find it difficult to follow David's example in Psalms 56 and 57, to confess our fear and then forget it? If you can, read Michel Quoist's prayer, The Delinquent, in *Prayers of Life* from which the quotation on page 94 was taken. Pray for the suffering people today.

5. Discuss whether your group might become more informed about some area of physical or mental suffering so that you can pray and help.

6. Why does the demand for justice figure so largely in the picture of the perfect king? What is the teaching in it for the church?

7. What injustices are there in our national life? Ought a Christian to be actively involved in fighting these (for example, in lobbying M.P.s, joining pressure groups; see notes on Psalms 58 and 66)?

8. Surrounded as we are by so many calls for action, how can we decide what we ought to do? What guidance does the example of Jesus give?

60 Encouragement in the Sanctuary

In Old Testament history God accepts .war, like divorce, polygamy, and slavery, as something that comes from man's 'hardness of heart', and from which he needs to be weaned. God declares that his purpose for mankind is permanent peace. Thus David was forbidden to build the Temple because he had 'waged great wars' (1 Chron. 22.8). There are many promises of peace (e.g. Isa. 11:1-10; Mic. 4:1-4), and Jesus Christ is the Prince of Peace (Isa. 9:6). Sadly enough wars still continue, but Christians, even when their country is at peace, know that the heart of all war is seen to be spiritual and is to be met by spiritual weapons (Eph. 6:10-17; Rev. 12:11).

The title of the psalm refers to events in 2 Samuel 8, where there is a catalogue of David's campaigns. It seems that while David was campaigning against the Syrians in the north, there was a defeat (1-3), not recorded in the history books, when neighbouring countries, Edom, Moab, and Philistia (8), invaded the country. Destruction over the countryside was not unlike an earthquake (1, 2), and the nation was reeling like a drunken man (3).

David pours out his heart in despair. Has God deserted the nation (1-3)? No, he is rallying his people round his standard to defy the weapons of the enemy (4). This last sentence is difficult to translate, but RSV is as good as any, together with JB, 'Hoist the standard to rally those who fear you, to put them out of range of bow and arrow'.

After a final prayer (5) David leaves his poem and goes into the sanctuary before the ark. In the silence God promises to restore the lands that had been overrun (6, 7), and to drive the invaders back to their own lands (8).

Before he leaves the sanctuary, David asks about Edom, which was probably the greatest threat. Should he invade it, in the light of Israel's defeat (9, 10)? David prays one final confident prayer (12), and with a declaration of faith (12), he hurries back to the palace to complete his poem. From 2 Samuel 8:13, 14 we learn that God answered David's prayer and gave him a great victory over Edom.

THOUGHT: David's sin with Bathsheba took place almost immediately after his victory over Edom. What lesson does this have for us?

61;62 Patterns of prayer

We need not look for any special occasion for these two pleasant psalms. We may treat them as prayer-poems that God moved David to write during his quiet times when he was not facing any specific tension. As such, they give us a pattern for prayer on 'ordinary days'.

There are times when we seem a world of distance from God, and yet in a moment we can talk to him (61:1, 2). As Christians we are often vulnerable, and need to find defence in God (2, 3). It is a grand thing to know that God is with us throughout the day, so that we can enjoy him as David enjoyed his communion in the tent that he had pitched for the ark (4; 2 Sam. 6:17). There is also the comfort of God's protective love (4; Matt. 23:37). From time to time it is good to look back over the course of our life to see how God has led us to inherit his blessings (5; Rom. 8:17).

It is natural for David to ask for a long life (6), for God has put in all mankind a desire for life rather than death, for healing rather than illness. Moreover the believer's long life is to radiate praise and dedication to God (8) as he rests in God's love in the place God wants him to be (7).

In Psalm 62 we note the occurrence of 'alone' and 'only' (vs. 1, 2; the same Hebrew word each time and in an emphatic position). Verses 1 and 2, 5-7 contain the same thoughts as 61:1-3. A new thought comes in verses 3 and 4, 9 and 10. Every day we encounter people whose life pattern is diametrically opposed to the way God wants for us. So here we have people whose envy turns into evil behaviour (3, 4), who are crafty, deceitful and hypocritical (4).

Verses 9 and 10 show the false values that these people have. Above all else they seek money (e.g. by extortion) and possessions, forgetting that rich and poor alike will be blown away at the hour of death. Contrasting with this are verses 11 and 12, showing God's values. We must draw upon his power and love, so that our actions match his requirements. This of course calls for self-examination.

THOUGHT: In these psalms there is meditation, request, confident faith and resolution. How are these reflected in your own prayers?

63;64 Night and morning with God

From very early times Christians sang Psalm 63 as a morning hymn because of the traditional translation of verse 1, 'early will I seek thee'. The Hebrew verb, 'seek early', is connected with the noun for 'dawn'. RSV, JB, and GNB paraphrase the verb as if it were a metaphor with the idea of seeking earnestly, and only AV and NEB keep 'I seek thee early'. In support of the literal translation we note verse 6, since meditation in the night prepares for seeking early in the morning.

This is yet another psalm written during David's outlaw period in the wilderness. The barren countryside reminded him of the barrenness of his soul without God (1). Even when he was an outlaw he was able to worship God in his sanctuary, for he visited Nob (1 Sam. 21:1-9) doubtless more than once and maybe Gibeon as well (1 Kings 3:4).

It is worrying to have the burden of sleeplessness, but, if we can quieten our mind, we have a further chance for quiet thoughts of God (6) which enrich the whole personality (5), and release faith for the day to come (7, 8).

We have previously read of the desperadoes who were hunting David down (57:4, 6; 59:1-7), and for them he sees only destruction (9, 10). Some treat verse 11 as a later insertion, but it is quite possible to refer it to Saul, whom David still treated as the Lord's anointed with divinely appointed duties to fulfil (1 Sam. 24:6; 26:9; 2 Sam. 1:14, 23).

We do not know the occasion of Psalm 64, but David once more speaks of his enemies (1-6). Doubtless he knew of conspirators and factions, who took sides with Absalom and other restless members of his family and court, looking for power.

David believed that God was the enemy of such people, and would show this by their collapse. Then bystanders would wag their heads in an 'I told you so' gesture, as some countrymen still do (8). By contrast, those who aim at God's standards are drawn out in praise to him.

THOUGHT: What can we learn from these psalms about openness to God?

65 A song for the harvest

For most of us poetry and nature are bound up together, and David as a poet was naturally moved by the wonder of creation. What he avoided was giving nature a capital N. Nature, God's creation, reflected the graciousness, glory, and power of God. We have seen this in Psalms 8, 19, 29, and we shall find a very long treatment in 104.

Meanwhile in this psalm David has the harvest in view, and his hymn glorifies the God who has given the harvest, thus fulfilling once again the promise to Noah (Gen. 8:22). We note the steps by which David comes to the climax. He probably remembers how the promise in Genesis is given in spite of the fact that 'the imagination of man's heart is evil from his youth' (Gen. 8:21). Thus he and his fellow worshippers begin their hymn of gratitude by coming with their sins for God's forgiveness (2, 3).

Only if there is forgiveness can there be access to God (4). All had access to the outer court of the sanctuary; the priests went inside; while only the high priest could go into the inmost shrine that held the ark, and that only once a year (Heb. 9:6-8). It was good to worship there (4), even though in David's day the sanctuary was still only a tent.

Although God manifested his presence in a special way in the sanctuary, he was very far from being confined there. Not only was he with his people in a crisis, but he was the one hope for the world (5). Now David takes up thoughts he has expressed in earlier psalms. He thinks of the towering mountains (6) and the seas that roar like thunder and are as quickly stilled (7). Perhaps with JB we should put a full stop after 'waves', and continue 'The nations are in uproar'. The storm-tossed world is awed by God's calming of the gales, and at the beauty of morning and evening (8).

At last David comes to the harvest, the crown of the year. Even though we count on the regular round of the seasons, this is by God's ordering, and we pray, 'Give us this day our daily bread', and thank God for providing it. The east especially values water after long dry periods, and David exaggerates this in verses 9 and 10, before he reaches his climax (11).

The psalm ends with vivid poetic images, starting with God driving through the land like a kindly overlord scattering largesse (11). Both agriculturalists and keepers of flocks are satisfied (12, 13).

THOUGHT: God gives most of us our harvest through our local greengrocer, baker and supermarket, and it comes from all over the world.

66 Joy after sorrow

Psalms 65-67 are a change from the run of persecution prayers. The joy of harvest (65) is followed by the joy of worship (66), and a call to the nations (67). Neither 66 nor 67 is ascribed to David but they could have been composed by him during his reign. Another suggested author is Hezekiah, from whom we have at least one psalm (Isa. 38).

An important part of the psalmist's worship is thanksgiving for what God did while his people were true to him. Then it was his enemies who had cause to fear (3, 4). In Psalms 78 and 106 we shall see how the nation turned sour, but they still had the stories of the wonderful deliverance from Egypt (5, 6) and the protection God gave from enemies who one by one had been subdued (7).

Yet protection had not been absolute, and the nation was now enjoying deliverance after a defeat. The psalmist sees this defeat not as punishment but as a test, which has bound them even closer to God (9-12). A nasty experience can be a warning, a punishment, or a test, and for the latter the Bible several times uses the picture of the refining of gold or silver in the fire. The silver is purified and shines brightly as the dross is removed by the fire under the pot (Isa. 48:10; Zech. 13:9; 1 Pet. 1:7).

When one's nation, local community or church face problems it is possible to feel that so many people are involved that one has no personal responsibility to do anything. But the psalmist, after including himself in the nation, accepts personal responsibility towards God. He had made his promises to God in his trouble, and, now that God has brought him through, he will not evade them (13, 14; Eccl. 5:4, 5). These include sacrifices of gratitude, of which he speaks in the language of a poet rather than a ritualist (15). The blessing was private, but his testimony is public (16, 17), and he is not boasting when he describes his own heart-searching as he came to God in prayer (18-20).

THOUGHT: The last two clauses of verse 12 make a good text for the wall and for life, and they sum up the psalm.

67 An invitation to come in

Although this psalm has a harvest background, it is essentially missionary. Anglican readers will recognise it as the *Deus misereatur*, which is an alternative to the *Nunc dimittis* at Evening Prayer. Its importance lies in its attitude to the nations. David, as we have seen, singles out certain enemies of God who will come under God's judgement. He assumes that some at least are so set in their ways that they will not turn, and the Bible certainly recognises that there are such people (Isa. 6:9, 10; Matt. 23:33; Rom. 1:18-25). Yet for those who repent God holds out his gift of mercy.

Some of the psalms similarly speak in severe terms of the nations round about, which were often a thorn in the side of Judah and Israel. Sometimes, but not always, they were agents of God to bring his people to their senses. Yet God's final word offers the prospect of salvation for others beside the Jews.

In Psalm 65 we saw that some would recognise the Creator behind creation, even though, as Paul found at Athens, they would be feeling after a God who was largely unknown (Acts 17:23, 27). Psalm 67 shows that the purpose of God's illumination of Judah and Israel (1) was that they should be missionaries to the nations (2, 3). There were already converts in David's day from the Philistines (2 Sam. 15:18-21), Hittites (2 Sam. 11:3), and Edomites (1 Sam. 21:7), and as time went on more and more were absorbed into the nation. By the time of Christ there were also many proselytes (converts), especially in Egypt. Now Christians have the commission to take God's final message of judgement and of glad salvation to the whole earth (4).

So the psalm sees the world ringing with the praises of Jew and Gentile alike. We know that the consummation comes with the return of Jesus Christ (Phil. 2:9, 10; 3:20-21), but even now there are his representatives in every continent, grateful to him for what he has done (5-7). We cannot overlook those whose sufferings dry up their praises, but their plight is taken up in other psalms.

THOUGHT: Should our invitation to others be one to join in our praise? What part does worship play in evangelism?

68 Praise to God

This exciting psalm is in a setting of God's triumphal march from Egypt to Zion and his enthronement in the Temple. It may have been composed for the bringing in of the ark to Jerusalem by David, since it opens with a quotation of Numbers 10:35 concerning the ark. All God's people are called upon to praise him, for he is powerful and glorious (4). He destroys the wicked (1, 2) and yet he is a kindly Father who looks after his family (5, 6). God's greatness is revealed by the stupendous triumph of the Exodus. David admires a fellow poet, Deborah, and happily quotes from her poem (7, 8; Judg. 5:4, 5). Curiously enough, both speak of the heavy rain at Sinai, which is not mentioned in Exodus, and this psalm takes up the theme of rain as a blessing (9, 10; see note on 65:9, 10).

The occupation of Canaan after various battles is described in verses 11-14. God speaks, it is done, and the women celebrate the victory (11, 12). The next two verses are obscure. A second parallel with Deborah in Judges 5:16 suggests that verse 13a blames any who refused to take part in the Lord's battles, while 13b describes the spoil that the women divided. But in the light of the sheepfolds quotation it could be a sarcastic self-estimation of the shirkers. Zalmon may be the place near Shechem (Judg. 9:48), but the main thought is that God's victories scattered kings like snowflakes.

Little Zion is more glorious than the great Mount Hermon in the hill country of Bashan, since the Lord has chosen it for his own (15, 16). He ascends the throne of his sanctuary there as his heaven on earth (17), and as conqueror receives the tribute of rebellious mankind (18). Inasmuch as the conqueror commonly distributes his tribute gifts to his followers, the verse is applied to Christ, who has ascended the throne as conqueror (Eph. 4:8).

While God saves his own people (19, 20), neither high mountain nor deep sea can save his enemies, and his people share his victory (21-23; poetry, not literal fact).

In the Temple procession (24-26) Judah and Benjamin represent the south, and Zebulun and Naphtali the north (27). When the Lord rules, other rulers submit, or are tamed like savage animals. Two examples are given: Egypt pays tribute, Ethiopia gives herself (28-31). Above all, the whole world is called to listen to God's voice, which should be heard through the witness of God's people (32-35).

THOUGHT: Without being untrue, this psalm expresses an ideal, just as some hymns celebrate the march of God in history, and his present and future rule.

69 Vicious attacks

Commentators tend to reject Davidic authorship here, and some suggest Jeremiah as the author. Although there is no time in the recorded history of David when we can easily place it, we may continue to regard him as the author. Previous psalms have shown how sensitive David always was to enemies. There are many years for which we have no record and there may have been much more unrest in the kingdom than we have imagined. As his sons grew up, others besides Absalom may have gathered cliques to unseat David from the throne, and this psalm could belong to one such time (NB, perhaps, verse 8).

The poet, like a drowning man, cries to God for rescue (1-3, 13-15). Something he has done has been misinterpreted, and has given a handle to his enemies (4, 5). His accusers have expressed surprise that a man of God should have behaved like this, and God's name is being dragged down in consequence (6-8). The more David has showed his earnestness, the more he has been mocked as a hypocrite (9-12). Yet he must continue to look to God as his only help (13-20).

In verses 21-28 David turns the tables on his enemies. They tried to poison him (21). Then they must feel the effects in blindness and inner agonies (22-24). They would drive David out; then they too must experience homelessness (25). They follow up any apparent signs of God's displeasure (26), and must incur God's perpetual displeasure on themselves (27). The parallel clauses in verse 28 show that the reference is to excommunication; they are no longer in God's book of his true followers (Mal. 3:16).

David takes no steps to actualise his prayer, but he knows God's pattern of 'The measure you give will be the measure you get' (Matt. 7:2). As Christians we sympathise with David's feelings, but we believe we should turn the other cheek, and leave God to act in his own way (Matt. 5:38, 39; Rom. 12:19-21).

The psalm ends in confident praise, with an addition for congregational use when the nation is in distress as David was (30-36).

The margin shows several New Testament quotations. Three are applied to Christ, though not as Messianic proofs. *a* Verses 4, 9. Unjustly hated: John 15:25; Romans 15:3. *b* Verse 9. Zealous for God's honour: John 2:17;

Two are applied to wicked men; *c* Verses 22, 23. Hardened hearts: Romans 11:9, 10. *d* Verse 25. A successor to Judas: Acts 1:20.

THOUGHT: What is the special relevance of this psalm to innocent people suffering terrorist attacks?

70;71 An old man remembers

Psalm 70 has been extracted from 40:13-17.

Psalm 71 is an interesting poem by a senior citizen (6, 9, 17, 18) who has become so familiar with other psalms that, like Jonah, he weaves them into his own hymn. It is worth listing these: *a* verses 1-3 from 31:1-3. *b* verses 5, 6 from 22:9, 10. *c* verse 13 from 35:4, 26; 40:14. *d* verse 15 from 40:5. *e* verse 18 possibly from 48:13, 14. *f* verse 19 from 35:10. *g* verse 24 from 35:4, 28, 40:14. All come from Books I and II, so presumably these psalms were being sung before the other books came into general use.

The theme is centred on God as the strong rock and the one on whom we can rely. It is extraordinary how often enemies are mentioned in the psalms, and it seems that godliness in itself drew the fire of those with different standards. Why else should anyone bother to attack an elderly citizen (7-11) and hold him up as an example of one whom God has discredited (7)? Perhaps prophets like Jeremiah were not the only ones whose rebukes roused the anger of those with lower standards.

The same may happen today, although more often in countries where Christians are very much in a minority but active in spreading the gospel with a call to repentance. The psalmist refuses to doubt God, but continues to praise him, and is resolved to go on talking about him as he has done from his youth (17-19). His old age may indeed be, as it were, new life from the grave (20).

So his gifts as poet and musician will be used in the service of God, whom he sees as the Holy One of Israel (22), a description which occurs only twice more in the Psalms (78:41; 89:18), although it is a favourite title throughout Isaiah.

THOUGHT: On the human level, in old age we are what we were all our lives, only more so.

72 The King as he should be

It is surprising that we have only two psalms ascribed to Solomon (72 and 127), since 'his songs were a thousand and five' (1 Kings 4:32), but some of the anonymous psalms could have come from him. We may compare this one with his father's estimate of a king in his old age (2 Sam. 23:1-7). David had groomed him for kingship (Prov. 4:3, 4), and doubtless what Solomon passed on to his own son (Prov. 1-9) he had learned from David. Although David and Solomon both had high ideals, both lapsed from them. David had a keen sense of guilt when he fell, but Solomon gradually deteriorated (1 Kings 11:1-13). However, the picture of the perfect king remained, and one day it was fulfilled in its essence – moral and spiritual perfection – by Jesus Christ.

One striking thing here is that there is not the slightest hint of battles, weapons, or violence, unlike Psalm 2. It appears that the world is drawn to the king by the essential goodness of his personality. Twice over he is seen caring for the weak and putting down injustice (1-4, 12-14). Solomon ruled the whole area promised to Abraham (1 Kings 4:21; Gen. 15:18), but he sees this kingdom as filling the world (8). He names representative countries from which wealth has come to him, Tarshish (perhaps Tartessus in Spain) and two countries in South Arabia (10), as typical of the wealth of the world (Rev. 21:26).

Jesus Christ has already won the right to be Lord of the world. When will his rule be open, as described here? Some see it as developing during the present gospel age, others as the millennial rule after Christ's return (Rev. 20).

It is interesting to note that the Anglican Prayer Book version of verse 4 is carved over the entrance to the Old Bailey, the central criminal court in Britain: 'Defend the children of the poor and punish the wrong doer'.

Notes. Some prefer to translate the title 'For Solomon', but the Hebrew preposition is the same as in other titles.

There is a difficulty over prayer for Christ (15), but the verse suggests a shout of 'God save the King!'

THOUGHT: Use the hymn, 'Hail to the Lord's anointed . . . ', a paraphrase of this psalm, in your worship.

Questions for further study and discussion on Psalms 60–72

1. Psalm 60 suggests no reason for David's subsequent disastrous moral defeat concerning Bathsheba. What reasons can you suggest for it? Do we have such experiences today?

2. '. . . First get free of that excess of goods which cram your whole body leaving no room for you and even less for God.' (Helder Camara, *The desert is fertile*) Do you agree that this should be a Christian's aim? Is this what Psalm 62 is saying?

3. What justification is there for harvest festivals (compare Psalm 65)?

4. How is God to be made known to the non-Christian world (compare Psalms 66 and 67)?

5. Work together on a montage to illustrate Psalm 68.

6. Discuss Romans 8:28 in the light of Psalm 69 and similar psalms.

7. How is Psalm 71 characteristic of an older believer? What are the special difficulties and privileges of old age?

8. To what extent do we defend the cause of the poor (72:4)? How do we fail? Compare a comment by Ruth Lister in the Guardian, February 1980, 'Progress towards eradicating poverty will be limited so long as politicians sense hostility or indifference to the poor.'

73 Solution in the Sanctuary

We assume that Asaph himself was the author of most of these psalms (1 Chron. 16:5), although 74 must be much later than the time of David, and would be by one of Asaph's descendants (2 Chron. 35:15; Ezra 3:10). The underlying theme of this group of psalms is the mystery, that we often feel, of God's apparent inaction. Psalm 73 states the problem and the ultimate answer in so far as we can receive it. We are convinced of the goodness of God (1), but are puzzled by the way the unbeliever gets on so well in the world, even when he openly defies God (9).

This misleads the average man, who enviously regards such people as living proofs of the irrelevance of God (10, 11). Why make the effort to keep up standards if God will not back us up when things go wrong (12-14)?

Asaph knew this temptation, but knew also that if he gave way he would be false to all that God had taught his people (15). So in prayer in the Temple he looked for some solution (16, 17). Here his eyes were opened to eternal realities, to God's ultimate verdict, sometimes seen in this life, but bound to be seen in the end (17-20).

In view of what follows we find a reference to the hereafter in these verses. The people of whom Asaph has been speaking are content with an animal existence, with only the body in mind (21, 22), whereas Asaph has the spirit link with God. This, unlike the unsubstantial dream of the earth-centred (20) is an introduction to the glory of the life to come (23-26). He sums up the facts in the two closing verses.

THOUGHT: Compare this psalm with 49. Both set out the aims and ends of the believer and unbeliever.

74 Solution in history

There is no situation in the lifetime of the Asaph appointed by David that corresponds to what is said here, but a descendant of Asaph, still known by his name, is living through a time of horror, which may well be soon after the destruction of Jerusalem by Nebuchadnezzar in 587 BC.

The remarkable thing is that this Asaph is more concerned about the suppression of worship than about the destruction of the city, which we have to assume. It is surprising that there were enemies who, like Jezebel of old, were so actively opposed to Jehovah that they tried to root out all centres of true worship (8). We know that after the fall of Jerusalem members of surrounding nations infiltrated into Judah (Jer. 49:1; Ezek. 25:2; 26:2; Neh. 2:19), and, before that, parts of Palestine had been already occupied by semi-pagan settlers (2 Kings 17:24, 33). Perhaps the newcomers saw that true worshippers of Jehovah would be a thorn in their sides, or else they wanted to score off Judah's God by proving him incapable of protecting his people (Lam. 2:17; Ezek. 25:8).

So Asaph turns to agonised prayer. He does not adopt the solution of Job's friends that all suffering is the exact recompense for sin, although in fact the biblical record shows that the destruction of Jerusalem was indeed a punishment for sin, to bring God's people to their senses. Evidently Asaph represents a God-fearing nucleus who had not gone into captivity nor into Egypt with other refugees, and therefore they could appeal to God with a good heart.

Looking back on history they could quote God's acts. They claimed the covenant redemption that he had given (2, 20), and through which he had saved them from the dragon, Egypt, and flung the drowned armies of the monster nation on the shore of the Red Sea for wild animals to devour (13, 14; Exod. 14:30). He brought water from the rock for his people (15; Exod. 17:6), and sent a drought on the land, as in the days of Elijah (15; 1 Kings 17:1). Finally, historical time began with God's founding of the universe (16, 17; Gen. 1:1).

Asaph's prayer was answered in fair measure. God worked in history, and after seventy years he brought back many exiles to rebuild the Temple (Ezra 1-6). Meanwhile the faithful loyalists took up their life in nearby villages, and continued to worship Jehovah as best they could (Ezra 6:21).

THOUGHT: How does a Christian plea correspond with the plea here?

75 Solution in waiting

The tune set for this psalm, *Do not destroy*, is taken from the harvest celebrations. We gather this from the occurrence of the same words in Isaiah 65:8, with the continuance, 'for there is a blessing in it'. This accompanies the gathering of the grapes. One wonders whether Asaph received his inspiration for the psalm when he took part in the singing as he gathered the grapes. His version is in verse 8, where the Lord's good wine is poured out, but the dregs are reserved for the wicked. It may be, however, that JB is right in its interpretation, '. . . frothing wine, heavily drugged; he pours it out, they drain it to the dregs, all drink of it, the wicked of the earth'. Jeremiah also used the acted parable of strong wine as judgement (Jer. 25:15-17).

Once more Asaph faces the problem of the prosperity of the wicked in spite of their clear defiance of God's revealed will (4, 5). The wicked are earth-centred, paying respect to anyone who is a 'big noise' or who throws his weight about like a savage bull tossing his head in the air (4, 5). All that matters to them is 'getting on', and they look in all directions for anyone of influence to back them (6).

They always overlook God. Yet when the time comes he will make his judgement clear (2). Meanwhile he works silently to keep society stable against the forces that would disrupt it (3). One thinks of Christ's words about how his people are the preserving salt of the earth (Matt. 5:13). The spread of the Christian faith has resulted in the gradual improvement of society, in the care of the sick, the treatment of prisoners, and the abolition of many social abuses.

This is one way in which God carries out verse 3. There is, however, the reverse of the picture. Where society is tottering (3), it is because of the standards of those who are denounced in the psalm.

Meanwhile we wait for God to intervene with his right judgements at his appointed time (2). Curiously enough a cup of wine is sometimes used as a symbol of judgement (8), perhaps because it can make the drinker insensible (Jer. 25:15, 16; Rev. 14:10). We throw up our heads with justifiable confidence as we praise the God with whom we are linked (9, 10). One day the sound of the saw will be heard on the horns of those whose self-confidence was not justified (10, N.B.4).

THOUGHT: Compare the thought of this psalm with 2 Peter 3.

76 Solution visible

The Septuagint Greek translation has a supplementary title, 'Against the Assyrian'. This is a likely occasion for the psalm, when the siege of Jerusalem by Sennacherib was miraculously relieved (2 Kings 19:35). This is also the theme of Psalms 46 and 48. It is interesting to consider why on this occasion God intervened in such a spectacular fashion. The Assyrian army was struck down by some form of quick-acting plague, similar to the plague of London or to the so-called Black Death (5).

The Assyrian attack was unprovoked, and was probably an attempt to extract fresh tribute. The king of Judah was Hezekiah, one of the few good monarchs. He called upon God for deliverance, and was assured by Isaiah that this would come (2 Kings 19:20-28), as indeed it did. No wonder that we have these psalms of celebration and gratitude.

The psalm builds up the picture of the majesty and omnipotence of God, and of his care for the weak against the strong. God takes the violence of men, and turns it to his glory, wearing it as though it were the girdle which makes a warrior ready for battle (10). The JB has a slightly different interpretation of the second clause of verse 10: 'The survivors of your wrath you will draw like a girdle around you'; NIV translates, 'are restrained'. Some amend the text slightly. Thus GNB has, 'Those who survive the wars will keep your festivals'.

These Asaph psalms represent the main ways in which believers have tried to understand the apparent silence of God when his people suffer. Down the ages Christians have kept their faith in God in spite of his silence, when outsiders have said, 'If there is a good God, why does he allow evil to flourish?'

We have seen some answers. Time spent in the sanctuary renews faith (Psalm 73). History shows that evil does destroy individuals and even nations (Psalm 74). We have the assurance that, even if we do not see God vindicating himself immediately, he has the last word in the final judgement (Psalm 75). Finally, we can all point to occasions when God has worked clearly and decisively (Psalm 76).

THOUGHT: When have I known this visible solution?

77 Guided bewilderment

The trouble about trying to find all the answers is that one argument seems to be upset by another. Here we find Asaph partly satisfied and yet still partly unsatisfied.

It is not easy to see what precisely is troubling him. It is not the prosperity of the wicked, as in Psalm 73. It does not seem to be a national disaster, as in Psalm 74. Perhaps it is a general feeling of depression, which is quite a common experience for Christians and non-Christians.

He is able to pray in the daytime (1, 2), but his mind is too active to allow him to sleep properly at night, or even to find consolation in meditation (2-4). Life is not as it was in the good old days (5), when he had a vivid sense of God's steadfast love (6-9). Life is gloomy, and God seems far away (10).

Yet, as often happens with vague depression, the clouds begin to lift and a patch of blue opens up. God turns Asaph's mind back to the great days of the nation; they were more than just 'good old days', they were days when God's hand was shown in strength as the situation demanded. Thus, it was an impossible project to bring the nation from Egypt to Canaan, yet God brought them in (11-15).

The miracle of the Red Sea (16) lifts Asaph's thoughts to God as the power behind nature (17, 18). Then he sees him as moving powerfully through the waters to his planned destination, leaving no trace behind him as men must. God knows where he is going (19). Then suddenly God is no longer the God of the storm and the waves, but the good shepherd (20). There is probably a significance in 'by the hand of Moses and Aaron'. God is certainly at work, but he commonly works through his servants. And is not Asaph himself one of these servants? Is he asking God to solve what he should be solving himself under God?

THOUGHT: 'I asked for strength that I might achieve. He made me weak that I might obey.'

78 Did we deserve it?

After all his gropings for a solution to the problem of suffering, Asaph sees that sometimes, though not always, we ourselves may be to blame if we do not respond properly to God's actions.

He begins with the glorious privileges of Israel, the privilege of being chosen and the privilege of having God's law for guidance (1-5). Each generation is called to share these privileges (6, 7), and the people are warned against the treachery of many of their forefathers (8).

The incidents that follow are obvious, except for verse 9. It may be that Asaph has in mind the occasion when some of the northern tribes failed to help Barak (Judges 5:16, 17), but he could be referring to some more recent unrecorded event.

All the incidents, which were occasions of God's love and help, were followed by a twisted response, which brought only punishment. Yet in spite of everything God brought his people to the promised land. Even here they chose unholy Canaanite god-substitutes for the Holy One of Israel (41), and earthly deities for the Most High God (56). Although the tabernacle and the ark had been set up in Shiloh (1 Sam. 1:3), God allowed the ark to be captured and Shiloh destroyed (60). Eli and his sons were killed (64. Also 1 Sam. 22:16-19). The nation suffered under the heavy hand of the Philistines (1 Sam. 9:16; 31:1-7), until once more the Lord let his power be seen and centred it in David and Jerusalem (68-70). Asaph sees the clouds clearing once more. The shepherd boy has been raised up to be God's under-shepherd of his people.

Note. Verse 2 is quoted of Christ's teaching by parables in Matthew 13:35, and the words are ascribed to 'the prophet'. Asaph was indeed a seer, or prophet (2 Chron. 29:30). The Hebrew translated 'parable' has a wide usage. A better translation here would be 'wise saying', 'instruction' or 'proverb'. This psalm describes the acts of God and the human response to them, from which spiritual lessons have been drawn down the ages. Thus in 1 Corinthians 10:1-11 the events of the history 'happened as symbols' and 'were symbolic' (6, 11, NEB). Christ's method of teaching similarly found symbolism in natural events.

THOUGHT: How many times have we said, 'I've learnt my lesson', or 'I'll never doubt God again after what he has done', and then . . .?

79 Desolate

This psalm almost certainly belongs to the time after the destruction of Jerusalem in 587 BC, and is likely to be by the same descendant of Asaph as the writer of 74. Both psalms read as though Asaph escaped before the captives were rounded up to go to Babylon (11), and is now trying to find some way of eking out an existence near Jerusalem. There is the same picture of utter desolation in 74:3-8 and 79:1-4. In each case Asaph's prime lament is for the ruined Temple, and he is concerned for God's glory and reputation. Here he pleads that the pagan nations may not find fuel to reproach the one true God. They taunt God, saying he is powerless to look after his own people (9, 10, 12).

We see the problem elsewhere. If God allows his people to sink morally and spiritually, the heathen will gain the impression that he cares nothing for righteousness. If, on the other hand, he sends, or allows, punishment to bring his people to their senses, the outsiders can say that he is not able to protect them, and has proved inferior to the gods of the conquerors.

Asaph asks forgiveness for the sins of the nation (8, 9), thus recognising that the exile is to be accepted as God's punishment. Yet there is still a problem. In Psalm 74 he merely prayed for relief, but in 79:6, 12 he asks for God's anger to be turned against the enemy. Such prayers are absent from the New Testament, and even in the Old Testament they are limited. Here Asaph thinks only of the peoples who have violently joined in with the Babylonians in massacre and destruction (e.g. Obad. 10-14; Zech. 1:15). He prays that God will act to show his anger at the acts of violence, and so demonstrate to those who do not recognise him that he has not forgotten his people.

We do not know how long it was before the answer came. God's punishment was not lifted instantly (Jer. 29:10), but eventually the king of Persia authorised the return from exile under a properly constituted governor (Ezra 1), and later Nehemiah returned with even stronger powers. The surrounding peoples were no longer able to claim jurisdiction over Judah, but were forced to admit Jehovah's power (e.g. Neh. 1:9, 10).

THOUGHT: How should I react when my 'sufferings' seemingly involve God's reputation?

80 The fate of the vine

The final compiler of the book of Psalms liked to group subjects together. Thus in Book I we had a set of David's outlaw psalms. Lately we have Jerusalem attacked and destroyed. One advantage of this grouping is that we see different reactions of the psalmist to a situation from which God seems to be absent. Few of us expect to see our homes in ruins, but we pass through wretched situations in which we long for God's intervention.

In the Greek Septuagint translation this psalm has an extra heading, 'Concerned with the Assyrian'. This connects with verse 2, which speaks of the northern kingdom of Israel, while nowhere is Jerusalem mentioned by name. Hence commentators generally refer this psalm to the destruction of Samaria by the Assyrians in 721 BC (2 Kings 17:6). If so, and if Asaph is the author and not merely a name for the collection, this must be yet another member of the famous family, perhaps on a visit to ruined Samaria.

Although 2 Kings 17:7-18, treats the destruction of Samaria as punishment for appalling sins, probably there were some godly survivors (see 2 Chron. 35:17, 18, 100 years later). Isaiah 5:1-7 reproduces the same theme of the vine that we have in verses 8-16, and includes both kingdoms, who have produced only wild grapes and must be rooted up. Other passages in Isaiah show that ultimately the vine of the nation will grow again, as Asaph prays here. Both Samaria and Jerusalem were restored, but the time of waiting was long.

Notes. Verse 17: the context suggests that Israel is the chosen man, but we read it with messianic overtones. The real joy for Israel will be restoration through Christ, who is God's true man.

FOR THOUGHT AND WORSHIP: let me give verses 17, 18 a Christian application.

Questions for further study and discussion on Psalms 73–80

1. In *the First Circle* Solzhenitsyn wrote of one of his characters, 'Thanks to his intense inner life, Nerzhin was free from envy'. How does Psalm 73 exemplify this?

2. How has the coming of Christ changed our outlook on the problem of the suffering of the righteous and the prosperity of the wicked?

3. In what areas of the world today do Christians experience the evils described in Psalm 74? Pray for these areas. Is there any other positive action you could take?

4. How does prayer help when God seems to continue to be silent (see notes on Psalm 76 and 77)?

5. 'God isn't interested in me.' 'I tried Christianity but it doesn't work.' 'He's not interested in anyone: look at all the suffering that goes on.' Do a role play of a discussion in which two people make these comments, and others answer.

6. Psalm 78 is an amazing recital of human ingratitude and rebellion. Yet we also so easily behave in the same way. Can you give any examples? Why do you think we are like this?

7. Psalm 78:5-8 talks of teaching the children to trust God. When and how do you pray with your children? What difficulties and blessings do you have as you try to teach children to trust the Lord?

8. Do you think children from Christian homes should be sent to church schools?

81 My way, not Thine, O Lord!

It is difficult to date this psalm, but it is likely to be well after the time of David, although disaster has not yet fallen on Israel.

It is festival time, either at the monthly occasions of the new moon and full moon (3), or at the new moon Feast of Trumpets (Num. 29:1) and the full moon mid-month Feast of Tabernacles (Lev. 23:39). Jewish festivals were linked to sowing and harvesting, but they also spoke of the deliverance from the bondage in Egypt (5-7). The strange line at the end of verse 5 has been taken to refer to the language of Egypt, but the RSV gives a different and more likely interpretation. Asaph, as prophet, hears the voice of God, different from the well-known voices of his friends. Thus the psalm now continues in the first person, as God becomes the speaker through the prophet.

Now that Asaph is not almost overwhelmed by disaster, God gives him a cool look at what inevitably underlies the process of history. The key verses are 11-13, with the old, old choice: whose ways; mine or God's? We cannot discover what would have happened if Israel had remained true to Jehovah instead of mixing up with the Canaanite deities and practices. We can only say that here we have God's promise of what he would have done, and indeed what he would still do (13, 14).

Asaph has been concerned about God's enemies. God here does not say he would destroy them, if Israel repented, but he would bring about their submission, even if submission were only nominal at first, as the word 'cringe' suggests.

Note. Gittith in the title is a tune, or instrument, from Gath, probably introduced by David. So also Psalms 8 and 84.

THOUGHT: 'I gave them over' (12). Consider this in the light of Romans 1:24, 26, 28. What happens if God withdraws? What relevance has this for a modern society?

82 Corruption in high places

As in Psalm 58, there are alternatives here. Who are the rulers whom God is condemning? A common view is that God is calling earthly rulers to account for their misrule. These rulers are given the title of gods (*elohim*) because they should be the representatives of God on earth. Certainly this is what the Bible teaches elsewhere (Rom. 13:1). Yet power is continually misused for selfish ends, and we join Asaph in crying out for God to overthrow unjust rulers and secure fair judgement for mankind (8).

The writer of these notes prefers the alternative view, that God is addressing spirit-beings who have taken control of the nations as their gods. In Daniel 10:13, 20; 12:1 we read of spirit-rulers of Persia and Greece, who are enemies of Michael, the unfallen guardian of Israel. It is likely that lesser spirits have set themselves up as gods and goddesses of tribes and groups, and missionaries have often said that the local spirits, who are worshipped and feared by the people, have a real existence, and resist the Christians through their influence over witch doctors and heathen priests.

The New Testament speaks of the Christian warfare against various grades of spirit beings (Eph. 6:12), but does not speculate on their names and powers as some Jews did and occult practitioners still do. Like Satan, they were created by God to minister in his service, but they rebelled and fell. They set themselves up as gods, but their destiny will be the same as that of rebellious man (6, 7).

One objection to this interpretation is Christ's quotation of verse 6 in John 10:34, 35, which appears to refer to men. What he actually says is that if, on the authority of the word of God, one accepts the title 'god' for certain designated rulers (whether human or divine), how much more should one accept the genuine title 'Son of God' for the one who has the unique relationship with the Father, such as Jesus had just claimed for himself in verse 30.

THOUGHT: Am I unduly influenced by Satan's standards in my treatment of others, especially if I am in a position of authority?

83 Background of history

This is the last of the Asaph psalms. There is no known, or likely, occasion when the peoples named in verses 6-8 made a concerted attack on Israel or Judah. Rather, Asaph is naming typical enemies who throughout history were always looking for a chance to obliterate the nation (4) and take their territory for themselves. Any of them might become the prevailing foe at any time. All that we can say about the date of writing is that it lies between the rise and fall of Assyria, 900-812 BC (8).

Israel's enemies are also enemies of the true God (2). Gods were bound up with the nations who worshipped them, and part of a victory was the degradation of the national god and his temple. Hence attacks were not just on the people of Israel, but on Israel's God (2).

Asaph's prayer is that these enemies will learn that Yahweh is not a national god, but the God of the whole earth (16, 18); this is also the Christian's aim. The people of God have always had enemies, and always will have to the end of the age. Often these enemies seem to win, but are never finally successful. Asaph looks back on history, particularly the time of the Judges, and finds assurances of what God can do.

He does not pray for the total destruction of God's enemies, such as they had planned for Israel (4). He is praying in strong picture form for such intervention as will lead to their conversion (compare verses 17, 18). The New Testament does not encourage us to pray for the death of God's enemies but for their submission to Christ through his victory on the cross so that they may be brought to accept him as 'the Most High over all the earth' (18).

Asaph's prayer was answered, but only after many years. By the time of Herod the Great most of these peoples were absorbed into Israel and in general accepted the Jewish faith. Even Tyre had its believers (Mark 3:8; 7:24-30). The peoples imported from Assyria (2 Kings 17:24) worshipped Jehovah as Samaritans. The Gospels and Acts show how the Christian message spread through the areas once occupied by the enemies of Judah.

Notes. Verses 6, 7: the Hagrites lived in Gilead (1 Chron. 5:10). Gebal was in Edom.

Verse 8: the children of Lot, i.e. Moab and Ammon, are included a second time as drawing strength from Assyria.

Verses 9-11: the references are to the battles in Judges 4, 5, 7, 8.

THOUGHT: Who are the Christians' typical enemies in the world today?

84 Return to the Temple

It is sensible to interpret this psalm as a sequel to the other Korah psalms 42, 43. There the psalmist was up in the north, and prevented from returning to lead the Temple processions once more (42:4; 2 Chron. 20:19). Now the opportunity has come to return. The Lord has dealt with him meanwhile, and now he would be willing to take the more humble duties of the Korahites, who also were doorkeepers of the Temple (10; 1 Chron. 9:19). His longing to dwell in the Temple was fulfilled, and he escaped at last from 'the tents of wickedness' (10; 42:10; 43:1, 2).

He describes the joy that the lover of God finds in the worship of God in the Temple (1, 2, 4). Even the birds have peace there. Sparrows, swallows, swifts, and martins (the Hebrew *swallo* could include all three) have always nested where man has built his houses, and in the precincts of the house of God they are not molested (3).

Pilgrims, with their hearts set on Zion (5), find the journey well rewarding. Even the dry places become springs of waters (6). *Baca* means *balsam tree*, which grows only in dry places. The psalmist spiritualises the journey. There are times when the presence of God seems very real, but the way may pass through dry places. As we find the springs and drink from the living water (John 7:37) we grow continually stronger (see vs. 6, 7). The final line of verse 7 is nowadays generally translated as in the RSV, but it is still possible to take it as the KJV, NIV and JB '. . . soon to be seen before God in Zion'.

Now the psalmist appeals to God to protect the king, Israel's shield and God's anointed (9). The KJV, NEB and JB make God the shield, as in verse 11, JB translating, 'God our shield, now look on us, and be kind to your anointed'.

The addition of 'elsewhere' (10) makes the meaning clear, and removes the misunderstanding which some readers have professed to find in the sentence, i.e. one day in church is preferable to many.

The psalm ends as it began with the joy of God's presence. The Temple by itself is only a rung of the ladder to fellowship with God himself (Gen. 28:12, 13, 17).

THOUGHT: 'They make it a place of springs.' How much emphasis should be put on 'they make'? Is it up to us to produce water in the desert?

85 Past, present and future

It is good to look back over the course of our life, especially when we can count our blessings. So the son of Korah looks back over the past to a period when God restored Israel from some disaster (1-3). His words do not suggest a major disaster, such as the exile, but it may be some tragedy that had happened during his lifetime. He admits that the sins of the people had brought it about, but God forgave them, presumably after their repentance.

Now some fresh trouble has come, and the psalmist prays that once more God may forgive the nation (4-7). He does not look simply for national restoration, but for revival that will lead to the enjoyment of God's love and salvation. This is a salutary reminder to the Christian church also. We all want the comfort of national security, but not all want inner revival.

Korah listens for God's answer. Like Asaph he may have had the gift of prophecy by which he could receive the direct word of God. God takes up his prayer (8, 9). He will indeed bring peace to those who open their hearts for revival, and his glory will fill the land. The last sentence of verse 8 has two renderings, but each has the same basic meaning. The RSV follows the Greek Septuagint translation, but points out in the margin that the Hebrew actually warns against going back again to the old ways. This fits well, and is followed by the KJV, RV, and JB ('if only they renounce their folly').

The final section describes the wonderful coming together of God's supreme blessings (10, 11). This may well be a foreshadowing of the Messiah, whose incarnation removes the barriers between heaven and earth, and whose Holy Spirit is poured into his people on earth. Meanwhile the land will be revived to enjoy the prosperity of good harvests, and God's people will follow in the steps of God's righteous standards.

THOUGHT: Read verses 10-13 alongside Isaiah 32:15-17.

86;87 The salvation roll-call

Psalm 86 contains fragments from various scriptures, but they are shorter than those in Psalm 71. One might compare it to the introductory prayer of a minister whose mind is stored with Scripture. There are too many quotations to list, but some Bibles have good marginal references. The fragments are not only from other psalms, e.g. verse 5 and Exodus 34:6; verses 8, 10 and Exodus 15:11.

This is the only David psalm in Book III, but with its quotations it does not read like the spontaneous outpourings of his other writings. It could be a kind of anthology of Davidic psalms, calling humbly on God (1-7), celebrating God's victories (8-10), not least in David's own life (11-13). Since David's psalms are marked by prayer for deliverance from persecution, this one closes in the same way (14-17). At the same time one cannot exclude David as author in later life, incorporating well-stored memories.

We may take verses 8, 9 as a missionary lead-in to Psalm 87. This psalm comes very near to the theme of Ephesians 3:4-6, where Gentiles are on complete equality with Jews as fellow-heirs in Christ. Other passages in the Old Testament speak of the conversion of Gentiles, but their exact place in the kingdom of God is left open (e.g. Isa. 19:24).

Psalm 87 looks forward to the end of the world. It is the Lord's roll-call of those who are members of the heavenly Zion (1-3). He calls the names of all who are reborn as citizens. What encouragement for missionaries! Old enemies of God are included (Rahab is Egypt) and the peoples call out their nationality (4). God welcomes each one as a citizen of Zion (5). In place of RSV there is another likely translation of verse 5; with a slight emendation based on the Septuagint; thus NEB, 'Zion shall be called a mother, in whom men of every race are born'; and JB, "Here so-and-so was born" men say. But all call Zion "Mother" since all were born in her'. This certainly brings out the grand theme of the psalm. It is followed by the Lord's enrolling of each one as someone born in the city of God (6), i.e. born again into the kingdom (John 3:3). Thus Rahab and Babylon are not saved because they are Rahab and Babylon but because they have become citizens of God's Zion. Obviously the reference is to the individual converts from all nations, not to the whole nation.

Let us praise God that the springs of our life are in the city which is alive with the life of God (7).

THOUGHT: Read Psalm 87 alongside Galatians 4:26, 27; Ephesians 2:13; Philippians 3:20, literally 'citizenship'; Hebrews 12:22, 23.

88 Depths of misery

When anyone is depressed and asks for music, he may not need a happy tune but could be helped by something more solemn. Similarly this rather depressing psalm is included for believers who are in darkness. Certainly Heman is passing through the depths. He is a drowning man who is just able to keep his head above water.

Companions might have helped him, but for some reason his friends did not want to know him (8, 18). Perhaps they believed, like Job's friends, that he was under God's curse for some sin that he had committed. (Job 30:9-11).

This was not the first time that Heman had suffered. He had known spells of illness all his life (15), and had constantly wrestled with death. As a wise man (see note) he looked at death under differing aspects. (a) Sheol, the state of the departed (3). (b) The pit, a standard word for a hole in the ground, and here probably the grave (4, 6). (c) Abaddon, ruin or disintegration of the body (11). (d) The shades. The Hebrew derives from a word signifying relaxed or powerless. They are without their material bodies (10). (e) Darkness, without the light of the sun (12; Job 10:21, 22). (f) Forgotten by man (12; 31:12).

In Old Testament times the state of the departed was seen as a negative existence, perhaps equivalent in its own way to hibernation. Death was the great enemy, as yet undefeated, and, compared with the activity of life with all its opportunities, existence without the body was a feeble and shadowy thing. For many non-Christians there is a similar gloomy outlook. It is noteworthy that Heman, at his stage of revelation, expects the answer 'No' in verses 10-12, but the new revelation in Christ has given a triumphant 'Yes'. Meanwhile Heman turns to God as his only hope (1, 2, 13), although on the face of it God might seem to be against him and indeed punishing him.

Note. Title: Heman the Ezrahite (i.e. descended from Zerah; 1 Chron. 2:6) was a wise man in the time of Solomon (1 Kings 4:31). Wisdom in itself does not free us from emotional distress. The sons of Korah put this psalm as an instruction (*Maskil*) in their collection. Another Heman, like the sons of Korah, was descended from Kohath (1 Chron. 6:22, 33). JB translates as 'Heman the native-born', as in Exodus 12:19, and the tune or title as 'In sickness or suffering'.

THOUGHT: The negativeness of death before Christ is treated also in Ecclesiastes 9:1-6 by another wise man.

89 The line of promise

Ethan was probably Heman's brother (1 Chron. 2:6), and was equally wise (1 Kings 4:31). In this psalm he also is concerned with death, and stresses its inevitability (48). He also knows what the insults of enemies mean (50, 51). Yet his alarm is over the afflictions of the king rather than over his own sufferings.

There is nothing to show when the psalm was written. If it is by a later Ethan, it is a cry after some disaster that has fallen on the city (40-43), although the language is hardly strong enough for the destruction by the Babylonians in 586 BC. If it was by the Ethan who lived in the time of David and Solomon, he may well be lamenting David's flight before Absalom (2 Sam. 15:13-17). If so, the picture in verses 40-43 is a metaphorical description of David himself, as verses 39 and 45 would suggest, so that the whole psalm concerns him.

The plea is based on the covenant and promise made by God himself (3, 4, 19-37; 2 Sam. 7; 1 Chron. 17:16-27). Now the promise is in jeopardy. David has been driven out (38, 44), and may shortly be killed (45-48). So Ethan reminds God of his covenant (49-51). He does this confidently, since he has such a magnificent view of the magnificent God (5-18). God rules over all in heaven and on earth. In heaven he is Lord of all spiritual beings (5-7), and on earth he is Lord of the raging oceans, by means of which he overwhelmed the Egyptians (Rahab) and saved his people (9, 10). He is the Creator of the world, north and south, and east and west (represented by the two mountains, 12). All true morality is grounded in him (14), and he draws out the worship of his people (15, 16). He has his representative on earth, the royal shield of the nation (17, 18), with whom the rest of the psalm is concerned.

The line of David was preserved for the coming of the great Son of David. Ethan was right to plead the promise. Thus verses 3, 4 are paraphrased in Acts 2:30, and the significance of 'first-born' (27) is brought out in Revelation 1:5.

So ends Book III with a double Amen.

THOUGHT: David's line was reduced to a mere stump in the ground and to a root in a dry soil, and yet the promise was fulfilled (Isa. 11:1; 53:2).

Questions for further study and discussion on Psalms 81–89

1. What difference of approach is there between the Asaph and Korah psalms?

2. Study Psalm 81 using the suggested Scripture Union questions: is there a command to obey, a sin to avoid, a promise to believe, a warning to remember, a positive example to follow, a principle to live by?

3. If Satan has set himself up as the god of this world (2 Cor. 4:4; Luke 4:6), how far does it help our understanding of events to know that his associates also try to influence smaller world groups (see notes on Psalm 82)?

4. Have you ever been in a position of responsibility? What are the special temptations and problems this brings? Pray for the leaders today in church, industry, education and government.

5. Is communism a deadly enemy to the Christian faith? Discuss Christian approaches to communism (compare notes on Psalm 83).

6. Rewrite Psalm 84 as if by a Christian today (compare Hebrews 9).

7. Try to express your vision of what it will be like when Christ comes (compare Psalm 85).

8. What are some of the divisions within us that stop us serving God sincerely and simply (86:11c, compare Jer. 32:39)?

9. Do you think that dance, mime and drama should be used in church worship (87:7)?

10. How can your church or group help the mentally retarded, the chronically sick, and the mentally sick?

90 'How great Thou art!'

The title indicates that this could be the earliest of the psalms. There are two other psalms by Moses, in Deuteronomy 32 and 33, and there are some resemblances between the celebrations of God's greatness in this psalm and Deuteronomy 32. If Moses was the author, he must have written this psalm while he was with Jethro, since he left there at the age of eighty (10; calculation based on Acts 7:23; Deut. 2:7; Deut. 34:7).

A single passage of Scripture cannot give us a total picture of God. In the Bible God reveals facets of himself at different times, and we do our best to view them as a whole. We generally find ourselves attracted to some more than others.

Thus we have here the enormous 'aboveness' of God, transcendent over space (2) and time (4), and short-lived man is as nothing before him (5, 9, 10). We may prefer the warmer revelations of God's character, yet there is surely room for something resembling the overwhelming awe that comes as we stand at the foot of great mountains. It is humbling and healing to see how small we are before God.

Life is a brief and hard pilgrimage (9, 10), and we need continual forgiveness for our sins (7, 8). We cannot despair, since, after all, the great God can guide us with his wisdom (11, 12). Now the gift of God's wisdom (12) gives a new perspective. All that has been said is true in the darkness, but how different it looks in the light of the morning (14). Yes, we have sinned, but God shows mercy for the past (13) and his love gives us positive cheer (14). Life may be short, and yet its days may have the compensation of God-given gladness (15). Instead of rubbish to be swept away (5), we may leave a building to the glory of God (16, 17).

Note. Joseph Smith, founder of Mormonism, turned the glorious poetry of verse 4 (2 Pet. 3:8) into scientific materialism. In one of his allegedly inspired books, *The Pearl of Great Price*, he states that God with a physical body lives beside a star called Kolob, which rotates on its axis once every thousand years in place of our earth's twenty-four hours.

THOUGHT: Compare this psalm with Psalm 39 and Isa. 40:6-8, 22-24.

91 The journey of life

This is a strange psalm. The outsider looks at the promises of verse 5-7, 12, and says, 'This just isn't so. Christians suffer like the rest of us.' Yet Christians in every age have taken this as a psalm of assurance of God's protecting goodness. As a simple example, it means that we cannot set out each morning with the fear that God has no plan for us, and that everything will happen to us by chance. We are in his hands, and look for his protection as we go on our way. We declare our confidence in the words of verse 2.

Even confidence by itself gives some protection. A doctor goes from patient to patient without constantly fearing infection, whereas a nervous person easily picks up one illness after another. When confidence is in God, so that it is backed by God, then verses 3-6 are of even greater significance. Today this includes protection from the dangers of the road, though these verses are meaningless if we ourselves drive without consideration for others.

There is a reminder in verses 7 and 8 of the basic division between the good and the evil, between those who can rightly claim to be on God's side and those who are against him. We shall see the recompense of both, maybe in this life, but certainly in the end. Again there come the tremendous promises in verses 9 and 10. We are travelling with God, and our home is where he is, in his secure place. Anyone who attacks us must first pierce God's defences.

The ministry of angels is spoken of in several places in Scripture. The special interest of verses 11 and 12 is their quotation by the devil when he tried to induce Jesus Christ to throw himself down from the Temple (Matt. 4:5, 6; Luke 4:9-11). Both Gospels show that Satan omitted the words 'in all your ways'. The promise is not for those who put God to the test in some spectacular way, but is for the day by day ways of the believer. For him there is victory as he tramples Satan underfoot (13; Luke 10:19; Rom. 16:20). The final verses show how all rests in God's hands.

THOUGHT: 'Whatever the need there is God's care and shelter to be found' (H. L. Ellison).

The next few psalms were clearly composed as hymns for singing in worship. The historical background is immaterial. The title of Psalm 92 shows that it was composed especially for Sabbath worship. Just as God completed his work of creation and rested on the seventh day, so he will one day complete his work of cleansing the fallen world before the eternal Sabbath. For this certainty, and the foretaste now, we praise him (1-4).

God's works in creation and history are there for the wise man to see, although the unwise supposes that a good time on earth is the main purpose of life (5-9). God's man throws his head up like the ox faced with enemies, and looks up while God pours healing oil on his head (10; 75:4; 23:5). He sees, as it were, through God's eyes, as evil meets its doom sooner or later (11).

We note the blend of poetry and spirituality in verses 12 and 13. The tree flourishes when its roots grow from the house of God. The fellowship of the Christian congregation should still be a source of nourishment for its members. Today, with increased life expectancy, verses 14, 15 are most relevant. Retirement is not a leafless winter.

Psalm 93 is one of several which open with the cheering declaration that Jehovah is King. His greatness and power are his royal robes (1). The very existence of the earth is proof of his creative power (1), and we worship him as the one who rules over all (2). Among the most terrifying forces on earth are the seas in a great storm. Their waves crashing on the cliffs hurl their spray to heaven, but, as in Genesis 1:6-9, God is master of the seas (3, 4; Matt: 8:26, 27). The scientific method is possible only because God's decrees, the laws of nature, are reliable (5). Happy is the scientist who is also a disciplined man of God (5).

FOR WORSHIP: Now that we have looked at a commentary, let us read Psalm 93 aloud as a song of triumph.

94 Yes to God's ways

Some psalmists are conscious of the thick fog through which they must grope to understand God's ways. This psalmist is more like a man on a summer's day, who puts a rucksack on his back and strides happily through the countryside and over the mountains. Like the girl in Browning's *Pippa Passes*, he sings, 'God's in his heaven, – All's right with the world!'

And yet, what about the clouds heavy with rain, the mists on the heights, and the stiff crags? The walker is inwardly prepared and adjusted to meet them. So the walker-psalmist strides out, inwardly confident in God, feeling that God is in charge. From the mountain he looks down on the plains from which he has come, where battles rage for the supremacy of false values. From the mountain he sees God at work, God assessing, God judging, and he gives his 'Yes' to God's ways (1-11). Moreover he can see into house after house, and knows there is a great host of witnesses, who are content to learn from their sufferings if only they may see more of God (12-15).

At the end of the day he is wonderfully refreshed. He has said 'Yes' to God, and knows that this means work for him to do on God's side (16). The day spent with the Lord has helped him to take a long, cool look at God's goodness in the past (16-19), and once more he takes his stand on the Lord's side against the wickedness of the world (20-23). He is not content with a 'Yes' view from the mountain which says, 'Let it be! It will all work out in the end'. God's work is his work also, and God's verdict is his.

THOUGHT: 'Whoso hath felt the Spirit of the Highest
　　　　Cannot confound nor doubt him nor deny:
　　　Yea, with one voice, O world, tho' thou deniest,
　　　　Stand thou on that side, for on this am I.'
　　　　　　　　　　　　　　　(F. W. H. Myers *Saint Paul*.)

95 Come!

Anglican readers know this psalm as the *Venite*, from the opening word in the Latin version, meaning 'Come ye'. So the psalm has been sung regularly by Christians as it was by Jews. The appeal 'Come' is immediately followed by 'let us' – an assurance of companionship (1, 6). It is often worth making the same appeal to friends and neighbours, with an offer to come with them.

Worshippers have always sung their praise and thanks to God (1, 2). Such singing should rise up to God in his majesty (3-5). Then we find ourselves back on earth, and our eyes close as we bow down in gratitude for our redemption. We were like sheep going astray, but now our Shepherd has found us (6, 7).

Worship is not a concert which we leave at the end of a performance. It binds us to the God who cares, and for whom we must care too. Listen to him with an open heart (7b). It is only too easy to get into a hard earthly rut, where our needs and wishes are all that count; where instead of our seeking God's way, God exists only to satisfy us. Note the transition from our appeal in 7b to God's words in 8. The two places, Meribah and Massah, mean appropriately 'Dispute' and 'Challenge' (8, 9; Exod. 17:1-7; Num. 20:2-13).

In verse 10 'I loathed' may be too strong. The NEB has 'I was indignant with', and the quotation in Hebrews 3:10 has 'I was provoked with'. Except for Joshua and Caleb the adult generation who came out of Egypt all died during the forty years before Israel entered the promised land (11).

It has become customary in some churches to omit verses 7b-11, although these are the verses that Hebrews 3:7 quotes as the words of the Holy Spirit. Hebrews 3 and 4 show once again that the Old Testament is to be read with a Christian application. Briefly, these chapters teach that the promised relief, or rest (*katapausis*), which has its fulfilment in heaven but which begins here on earth, is also a Sabbath rest (*sabbatismos*, 4:9). We no longer struggle to put ourselves right with God by our own works (4:9, 10), yet we strive to live our lives hearkening to his voice (3:13; 4:11).

THOUGHT: Note the application in Hebrews 3 and 4, especially 4:6-11.

96;97 Great is the Lord

We have noticed before that some sequences of psalms take up a similar theme. In the group that follows the psalmist abandons himself to praise of the one and only God, who is the Lord of all the earth (96:1; 97:1). Those who know him proclaim him to all the world (96:2, 3).

Most of us know nothing of what it is like to be surrounded, as the psalmist was, by pagan high places, and to find even more gorgeous heathen temples on visits to, or exile in, foreign lands. There are still some parts of the world where the situation is like that today. Each holy place has its idol, which in practice is treated as the patronal god or goddess. Yet how can a thinking person bow down before these 'worthless idols' (97:7; 96:5; Rom. 1:22, 23)? Whatever realities may be behind them (see, possibly, Psalm 82), they in their turn must bow in submission before Jehovah (97:7, 9).

So the glory song goes on (96:6-9), celebrating the wonder of creation (96:11, 12; 97:2-5), and calling a multitude of others to true worship (96:9). The opening words of the hymn, 'O worship the Lord in the beauty of holiness', are quoted from the KJV of 96:9, which here is followed by the NEB with 'in the splendour of holiness', and there is much to be said for this rendering of the Hebrew. Certainly it must mean more than Sunday best clothes.

Holiness naturally needs to be defined if it is not to be identified with mere piety, and it is worth studying with the help of a concordance. Since 'without holiness no one will see the Lord' (Heb. 12:14), it is not surprising that the psalmist's thoughts turn to God's final assessment of mankind (96:10, 13). This will be 'with equity', 'with righteousness' and 'with truth' (96:10, 13). Meanwhile in this life we have a foretaste of God's judgements (97:8), and we travel through life seeking to be on God's side, and knowing that our lives are in his hand (97:10). The light grows brighter until the true sun rises with the eternal dawn (97:11).

THOUGHT: The hymn 'O worship the Lord in the beauty of holiness' contains some of the themes of these psalms. Use it as an aid to your private worship.

98;99 Mighty King

After all the struggles that we have been through in some of the psalms, it is wonderful in this group to come to the only possible climax of world history, the ultimate universal realisation of God as the supreme King. There have been many battles, but now comes the victory (98:1-3). At last all acknowledge him as the wholly righteous and all-loving God (2, 3).

When even in this life we see him 'in a mirror dimly' (1 Cor. 13:12), we cannot help anticipating the eternal praises (4-6) when the restored creation (Rom. 8:21) adds its voice (7, 8). If we think it out, are we not longing every day for righteousness and equity in political and social life, but only too often fail to find it? Yet could we ourselves sometimes be responsible for failure?

Psalm 99 tears the veil aside and shows us God in heavenly glory. The cherubim over the ark in the holy of holies (Exod. 25:18, 21, 22) were earthly symbols of the spiritual host around the heavenly throne (99:1; Ezek. 10:1; Rev. 4:6-8, where comparison with Ezekiel shows that the living creatures are cherubim). Once again in this psalm the mighty King vindicates all that he has done (4, 5), and draws out praise and worship (3, 5).

We, too, may prove God's love and power in this life as men of God proved them in past history (6). Although these men needed forgiveness for many things, as also do we, and indeed suffered, as Moses and Aaron suffered in not being allowed to enter the promised land (8), yet their hearts (like ours?) were set on obeying God, and again and again proved that he answers prayer (7).

Note. Verse 6. Moses was priest before the line of Aaron was set aside for this duty (Exod. 24:6-8), and Samuel offered sacrifice after Eli and his sons had been killed (1 Sam. 7:9).

THOUGHT: Let us ask for an inner vision and awareness of God, that we may be drawn out in praise (98:5) and worship (99:5).

Questions for further study and discussion on Psalms 90–99

1. Psalm 90:3-12 suggests that man's life is unhappy and meaningless. How do verses 11-17 answer this?

2. Discuss Psalm 91 in the light of 1 Corinthians 4:9-13 and 2 Corinthians 4:7-12.

3. How are we to explain the generally acknowledged weakness of our worship? What can we learn about the reality of worship from the worship psalms in this section?

4. The Lord is in heaven and also on earth. How does a Christian bring these two facts together in experience?

5. 'People today try to get away with all they can. When I try to do what's right I stand out like a sore thumb and it causes no end of trouble.' Do you agree with this comment? When do you find it particularly difficult to follow justice scrupulously (94:15. See also notes on Psalm 98)?

6. What is the difference between holiness and piety (see notes on Psalm 97)?

7. What reasons does Psalm 98 give for praising God? What would you add? Have a time of prayer, each member of the group praying one sentence beginning, 'I praise you, God . . . .'

8. What does the psalmist mean when he says, 'Thou wast a forgiving God to them, but an avenger of their wrongdoings'? Can you find similar contrasts in the New Testament?

100;101 Lips and heart

Psalm 100, which Anglicans know as the Jubilate (rejoice), continues more or less the theme of the last few psalms. It is true that there is no mention of the final manifestation of God in judgement, but he is certainly experienced by his people as the one wholly worthy of praise. Indeed we call upon the world to know him in the same way (1).

To him we owe our creation and preservation (3), and for these we thank him, not simply in the quiet of our own hearts, but unitedly with all others who have known his goodness (4). This is one reason for our coming together on the Lord's Day. Again, the closing verse brings us back to the great goodness of our God.

Psalm 101 has a totally different ring about it, yet one can see how appropriately it follows on. There is always a possibility in some services and meetings of letting ourselves go in singing catchy choruses and stirring hymns. There is much to be said for expressing praise in song, although different people find different types of music most helpful. Yet it is easy to be carried away with legitimate emotion, and then to forget the other service of God in day by day life. Hence Psalm 101 brings us back from the glory to the everyday walk.

The psalm is obviously by a man who can influence others. As God's representative on the throne David tries to keep God's standards in front of him. Hence his attitude is both negative and positive. He will oppose evil (3-5, 7, 8) and encourage all who stand, as he does, for God and his ways (6). He is concerned that his gospel shall be social as well as worshipful.

Note. In verse 3 the translation 'and not we ourselves' (margin and KJV text) in place of 'and we are his' (KJV margin and probably all modern versions) depends on two possible translations of the Hebrew *lo*, as *not* or *to him*.

THOUGHT: There are two well-known paraphrases of Psalm 100, 'All people that on earth do dwell', and 'Before Jehovah's aweful throne'. Notice how closely they represent the original.

102 Causes of depression

In an earlier note we saw that when a person is depressed it is useless to try to jolly him or her along with bright thoughts or lively music. A psalm of this kind gives an outlet for sadness, as the title suggests. The full title is significant: the one in despair 'pours out his complaint before the Lord'. He is not a mere grumbler. To be able to talk constructively to someone who understands is half the battle.

The psalm is worded to cover a wide scope, and it is impossible to pin the reference to one single form of suffering. In this way it resembles Paul's vague reference to his 'thorn in the flesh' (2 Cor. 12:7), which Christians have applied to various personal afflictions.

A study of the psalm shows certain well-known grounds of depression: no sense of God's presence (1, 2); a gloomy feeling that death is near (3, 11, 23, 24); sheer physical pain (3, 5); loss of appetite (4); loneliness (6, 7); a lack of sympathy (8; people wonder what wicked thing he has done to bring God's curse upon him, contrast Gen. 12:3). The dust he has thrown on his head to indicate his distress (e.g. Josh. 7:6) has fallen into his food to be mixed with his tears (9). He bears the weight of all that is tragic in contemporary society (14).

He feels that somehow God is to blame for all that is happening (10), and yet he still has enough faith left to turn to God as his one hope (1, 2). There is no final end to his depression except the vision of God on high and of the final setting right of all that has been going wrong (16-22). What a contrast between depressed man, with his short life, and the eternal God, Creator of heaven and earth (12, 25-27).

In Hebrews 1:10-12 the application of verses 25-27 is made to the Lord Jesus Christ. There is no doubt that these verses speak of Yahweh, but Yahweh creative is the second Person of the Trinity, the Lord Jesus Christ (Col. 1:16; Heb. 1:2). Using this psalm a Christian travels on to the further revelation in and through Jesus Christ. Not only is he the Creator, but he also involved himself in his creation, including its depression, as in Gethsemane, on his way to redeem us on the cross.

It is wrong to suggest that one or two readings of this psalm will cure all depression. Depression may have physical causes, but this psalm is a reminder that there is no absolute cure without God.

THOUGHT: Consider the value of talking to God about our depression or other troubles.

103 Good cause to be happy

What a delightful contrast to follow the depression of Psalm 102! This is another psalm for shouting aloud with joy. It has everything that we need, both positive and negative. It is good to see David as the author. We have shared with him in his struggles and persecutions, and now we share with him as he opens up joyfully to God.

Nothing could make a better opening for a new day than the spiritual explosion of verses 1 and 2. The sins of the past, that would have pulled us down, have all gone (3) – a glad realisation that comes more than once (8-12). The Anglican Prayer Book describes us as 'miserable' sinners, but this is the old fashioned use of the word, meaning 'pitiable', i.e. dependent on God's mercy, and this is brought out in verse 13. Once forgiven and redeemed, we have no reason to be miserable in the sense of the word today.

In verse 3 we have the same problem as in 91:3-8. God does not give a hundred per cent deliverance from illness, and in fact more psalms lament over sickness than rejoice in health. Yet illness often has its roots in wrong-living, so that the resistance of body and mind is slacker. Then we need repentance and God's forgiveness to restore health. Indeed a close walk with God is normally the way to all-round renewal (5). In any case it is right for most of us to go through the day with the confidence of verse 3, that God will keep us from infection (see notes in first two paragraphs of Psalm 91). Yet there are some illnesses and physical sufferings that we share with fallen humanity and which are not due to personal sin, e.g. Paul's thorn in the flesh (2 Cor. 12.7).

It is striking that the psalm which shows a believer on the crest of life should also have a reminder of his frailty (14-16). It is the sheer joy of contrast between nature and grace that means everything to the Christian.

The concluding verses lift us up to God in his supreme majesty (19-22). We are talking of relationship with him, not a happy humanist philosophy.

THOUGHT: Consider this psalm as an exposure of sin, forgiveness, and the new life.

104 For nature lovers

Many writers have been moved by the beauties and wonders of nature. Today we marvel at the detailed natural history films on television. Although the speakers may ascribe everything to 'nature', common-sense sees the creative mind of the one God, who loves infinite variety, as indeed we ourselves do.

Scholars have remarked on some similarities between parts of this psalm and an old Egyptian poem in praise of the sun as the supreme god. This was composed in the time of the monotheist (or maybe monolatrist) Pharaoh Akhenaten, about 1350 BC. This does not raise a problem about inspiration any more than do similarities between the laws given to Moses and the social laws of contemporary civilised peoples. Whether or not this poem was known in Israel through Egyptian bards, this psalmist challenged it by passing beyond the sun to the Creator of the sun, the universe, and all that is in it. So also Psalm 19:4-6.

Not only is God the Creator (1-9) but he is the conserver (10–35). Already the psalmist has seen what we see in television programmes in closer detail – the links between the created order (10-23). Each part of the universe depends on other parts, and in turn is a link for others. Man shares in the links as a conservationist (14, 23) and as a beneficiary (14, 15).

The sea is not forgotten, with its fish (25), its trading vessels (26) and its giant monsters like the whale (26). It is pleasant to note the variant translation here in the GNB margin and the JB, 'the sea-monster you made to amuse you', or the NEB, 'whom thou hast made thy plaything'. God surely has a sense of pleasure (31; Gen. 1:31), and did not create everything for bare utilitarian reasons. If one has time, it is worth comparing this psalm with God's description of creation in Job 38-41.

We are reminded that the breath of life is a loan from God. All individual creatures die, but the race is continually renewed (29, 30).

Yes, God is joyfully supreme, and nature may be a ladder of praise to him (31-34). Unfortunately some 'nature worshippers' stop on the ladder, and so miss the joy of relationship with the personal God, who cares about sin and forgiveness (35).

Note. Verse 4: the translations here and in Hebrews 1:7 vary because angel and messenger are the same word in Hebrew and in Greek, as also are spirit and wind.

THOUGHT: Can one gather from this psalm that God enjoys his creation? Does Jesus Christ also show enjoyment (e.g. in his parables)?

105 God's potential

Psalms 105 and 106 are striking contrasts of the potential and the actual. In Psalm 105 God is the deliverer, but in Psalm 106 Israel continually defies God. In Psalm 105 we tell of the glory of God in history, just as in Psalm 104 we told of his glory in nature. God's blessing is linked to the covenant that was first made with Abraham, and renewed with Isaac and Jacob (6-11, 42). We also share in this covenant, in Jesus Christ, the promised offspring of Abraham, as is closely argued in Romans 4 and Galatians 3. We also have known deliverance from an Egyptian bondage.

The psalm, which was composed by David and used in part when he brought in the ark (1 Chron. 16:8-22), surveys Israel's history, showing how God protected the patriarchs in their wanderings (12-22). In verse 15 they are spoken of symbolically as God's anointed chosen, and, inasmuch as each had direct communication with God, which was the mark of a prophet, they are here designated 'prophets'.

In verse 18 it is sad to lose the striking phrase, 'the iron entered into his soul', which has become a familiar metaphorical saying in English. Modern translations prefer a rare use of *nephesh* as neck in place of the usual soul (e.g. Psalm 69:1), and the context suggests this meaning here for the literal translation 'into iron went his *nephesh*'.

Not all the ten plagues of Egypt are listed (27-36), and the psalm does not keep the chronological order. Unlike the psalm that follows, this contains no hint of rebellion in the wilderness, but tells only of God's miraculous provision (39-41), culminating in the promised entry into Canaan (43, 44). Ultimately Israel must not live on miracles, but on the word of God (45). The giving of the law on Sinai has not been listed earlier, but its codifying of the word of God in a form of statutes and laws is both a rounding off of this psalm and a preparation for the next.

THOUGHT: How much does a miracle achieve for faith and behaviour?

106 Man's realisation

In Psalm 105 we saw all that God did, and was prepared to do, for his people so that they might follow his ways, and thus enjoy life in its fullness. In the general introduction to these notes we noticed that a psalmist may write from one angle, and leave it to others to balance the truth from another. Thus in Psalm 105 we have God's potential, while here, as in Psalm 78, we have the people's actual response.

The psalmist is concerned because of his identity with his people in their blessings and their sin (verses 4, 5, 6). By recounting the cycles of need, deliverance, falling away, punishment, restoration, he asks where they stand at the present time. Has the nation learned anything from history since they were delivered from Egypt and brought into the promised land?

It was strange to find the people attracted to Canaanite gods and goddesses, even to the extent of sacrificing their children (37, 38; Jer. 7:31). They exchanged the glory of God for debasing images (20; Rom. 1:20-23). A further attraction was the indiscriminate sex at the Canaanite high places (39; Jer. 3:6-10).

It is not easy to understand the command to destroy the Canaanites (34; Deut. 7). One can say that the order was not given in isolation, but in relation to the effect that the Canaanites would have on the worship of Jehovah. In a strange unity between man and nature, Canaanite degradation even polluted the land (38; Lev. 18:24-30). The Canaanites remained, and the result was a complete breakdown of God's purposes as given in Psalm 105:45. Yet there was a door open for the conversion of individuals like UrIAH the Hittite (IAH is an abbreviated form of Jehovah – showing either his own or his parents' allegiance).

Other sins besides those of idolatrous worship pulled the nation down, and God recalled his people to their senses by suffering, which might go so far as subjugation (41, 42) and eventually exile. But always there was the opportunity of repentance, followed by restoration (43-46). So the psalmist, seeing the nation once more brought low, lifts up his heart to God. Maybe not all will repent, but he at least will act as the nation should.

Book IV closes with a doxology, as do the other books (41, 72, 89, 150).

Note:– verse 38, Christians with a gift of discerning of spirits say that centres of evil worship may remain polluted by an atmosphere of evil.

THOUGHT: What modern 'Canaanites' are a danger to the church?

Questions for further study and discussion on Psalms 100–106

1. What do we mean when we talk of the goodness of God (100:5)?

2. How would you answer someone who says, 'I don't want to go to heaven; it would be so boring'?

3. Ezekiel 18:5-9 describes the standard of righteousness for God's people. Compare this with the description in Psalm 101. How would you summarise these?

4. Of the passage in Ezekiel, Howard Marshall writes, 'It is reasonable to suppose that the particular prohibitions and commands listed reflect those areas where Ezekiel's contemporaries most especially needed to be reminded of the nature of justice, and that a different spokesman in a different situation might have underlined other, equally important, commands.' Write out your own psalm, describing the righteous man today.

5. What do humanists believe? What is the difference between humanism and Christianity (see comment on Ps. 103)?

6. The Scripture Union soundstrip *In the Beginning* is a beautiful commentary on Psalm 104. It can be used to introduce a devotional evening of meditation and worship. There are also discussion questions.

7. Compare Psalm 104 with Job 38 and 39, and draw out the differences of approach. To what do you attribute them?

8. Central to Psalm 105 is the covenant (7-11). What did this mean to the Jews and to the New Testament Christians? What does it mean to you today? (Compare Jeremiah 31:31-34; 1 Cor. 11:25; 2 Cor. 3:6; Heb. 8.)

9. What is the difference between Psalms 105 and 106?

10. Have you experienced miracles in your life? If so, in what ways has this helped you? What are the limitations of miracles? When do you think it is right to pray for miracles?

107 Crest and trough of the wave

This psalm has closer links with Psalms 105 and 106 than with Book V in general. Psalm 105 gave us the crest of the wave, Psalm 106 the trough. This psalm links the two concepts, and shows how God has lifted up people who were down, even when the downfall was their own fault. It presents four dramatic situations in which the members of the redeemed community find themselves (1-32), followed by a general conclusion (33-43).

a Verses 4-9. Travellers have missed their way as they journey to the city. They are desperate for food and shelter as they wander in circles in the barren wastes. They call to God for help, and he responds by leading them straight to their destination. There follows the chorus of praise, which is adapted and repeated at the end of each section. The pictures are likely to be spiritual illustrations. Thus here we think of Isaiah 35:5-10 and Hebrews 11:13-16.

b Verses 10-16. The next group are in bondage through their own fault. They have defied God, and consequently are prisoners away from the light. Again a heart cry to God brings them to freedom. The picture is typical of the bondage of sin, as in Isaiah 42:7 and Colossians 1:13.

c Verses 17-22. Another picture of sin, this time as the sickness that destroys. Gone is the appetite for life, and only a steady drift towards death remains. Again there is the same way out, the only way. We think of Isaiah 53:5; 55:2; 57:18, 19; John 6:34, 35.

d Verses 23-32. Here we are in the storms of life, not shirking the call of duty, but finding ourselves battered by the waves of one trouble after another. It is not our fault, but there comes a point when we realise that our own ability is not sufficient. Once again we cry to God. This storm picture is not common in the Bible, since the Jews on the whole were not deep-sea mariners. Perhaps one might compare Isaiah 25:4 and the experience of Mark 4:35-41.

The closing sections are more general, and lack the refrain. Verses 33-38 amplify the pictures in verses 4-9, while verses 39-43 give the typical reversal of human ups and downs, as in Luke 1:51-53.

THOUGHT: Does a spiritual application make these pictures any less real?

108;109 A blessing and a curse

Psalm 108 combines two psalms on which we have already had notes, i.e. 57:7-11 and 60:5-12. When David wrote 60:5-12 he had an actual campaign in mind. The editor who included the section here was probably visualising the 'Moabs', 'Edoms', and 'Philistias' that the average worshipper had to face. He was applying the history just as some of our hymn writers apply the lessons of the wilderness wanderings, 'Glorious things of thee are spoken' and 'Guide me, O Thou great Jehovah'.

Psalm 109 belongs to one of David's illnesses. Several psalms suggest that he was subject to attacks that laid him low, and these formed opportunities for conspiracies by his enemies, often from parties in his court. We have an indication of parties centred on Absalom (2 Sam. 15:1-6 and Adonijah (1 Kings 1:5).

It is possible to read this psalm as a thoroughgoing curse on David's enemies. Another interpretation treats verse 6 as the words of David's enemies which David quotes in verses 2-4 and 28.

The JB and the NIV margin have this, and the NEB moves towards it. The question, is how far do the curses of the enemy run? The NEB puts verse 6 alone in inverted commas, while the JB includes verses 6-15. There is no reason why the enemy's words should not go up to verse 19 (NIV margin). What is said about David is not true, but it is human nature to exaggerate charges against those we hate, and the idea here is to build up a powerful curse which will move God to destroy David.

David's reply, in effect, is to say, 'If this is what you think is good for a fellow human being, then presumably you would like to experience it yourself' (20, 28, 29). Meanwhile he calls confidently on God, and knows that he will be restored to confound those who wish him dead. Note: Verse 25, To wag the head is a sign of disgust.
Traditionally in Britain a person shakes his head and says 'How shocking!' (See also Jeremiah 18:6, Lamentations 2:15; Psalm 22:7; Matthew 27:39.

THOUGHT: It is only too easy to exaggerate other people's faults when I fall out with them.

110 The ascended Lord

There is no doubt about the importance of this psalm. The first verse is quoted and paraphrased in the New Testament more often than any other Old Testament verse.

Jesus Christ's quotation of it would be meaningless unless David were the author (Matt. 22:41-46). Moreover, Jesus declares that the 'lord' referred to is the Messiah, and the Jewish authorities accept this. David speaks of one greater than himself as his lord. This does not mean that the Messiah is not also his descendant, but that Jesus says that he is not *only* his descendant.

Other quotations in the New Testament naturally refer verse 1 to the ascension, when Jesus Christ returned to the central place of rule in the universe. By his death and resurrection he gave the death blow to the Lord's enemies, Satan, sin, and death, and now he is asserting his victory in and through his people. The enemies are still there, but they cannot deny the rule of Jesus Christ exercised from the Jerusalem which is above (2; Heb. 12:22-24). On earth we his followers are not puppets, but we have a magnificent leader with the vigour of youth whom we should follow freely (3).

The margin shows that there is some uncertainty over the exact translation of verse 3, and the NEB, JB and NIV refer the whole verse to Christ. Thus the NIV has, 'Arrayed in holy majesty, from the womb of the dawn you will receive the dew of your youth.'

The significance of the Melchizedek promise is argued in Hebrews 5-7. Melchizedek appears suddenly for one moment on the pages of history as king-priest in Jerusalem, without anything being said of his parentage or subsequent death or any successors (Heb. 7:3), and so is quoted as a picture of the eternal Messiah. Hebrews does not explore the life of Melchizedek but draws its application from what is actually written, and omitted, about him in Genesis 14. Nothing is said in the story of human antecedents nor of a successor in the priesthood. So Christ, having offered the final sacrifice for sin, has no successor as the Levitical priests had, but is priest for ever as the psalm says (Heb. 7:11-17).

The final judgement is described in terms of a war to end all wars (5, 6), but the psalm concludes with a beautiful picture of refreshment in the heat of battle. We also are not left thirsty without the living water that our Saviour gives (John 4:13, 14; 7:37, 38).

Note. The name of Melchizedek was specially significant to David since he had recently captured Jerusalem.

THOUGHT: 'Let us hold fast the confession of our hope without wavering, for he who promised is faithful' (Heb 10:23).

111;112 To be like him

These two psalms are both in the acrostic or alphabetic form, and each half verse, apart from the opening Hallelujah, begins with a fresh letter of the alphabet. The JB sets this out.

Hallelujah, which is the Hebrew word translated 'Praise the Lord', is very much a part of our Christian vocabulary. Yet in the Old Testament the word occurs only in this part of the book of Psalms, either at the beginning or end, i.e. 104-106; 111-113; 115-117; 135; 136; 146-150. In the New Testament it occurs only in Revelation 19:1, 3, 4, 6. Hebrew or English, it is a fine word to clear the spiritual lungs.

The two psalms balance each other. Psalm 111 sets out the revealed character of God. Psalm 112 balances this by showing how we may be like him. One commentator calls Psalm 112 'a holy parody' of Psalm 111. Thus, for example, 'his righteousness endures for ever' is said both of God and of his follower (111:3; 112:3, 9). The Lord is gracious and merciful (111:4), and so is his follower (112:4 according to NEB, JB, GNB, NIV, and RSV margin). The Lord is generous (111:5), as is his follower (112:5, 9). The Lord is trustworthy and just (111:7), and so is his follower (112:5).

Both psalms give the proper response to God and his goodness. Praise and thanks are an emotional reaction (111:1); study is an intellectual approach to revelation (111:2), although intellect by itself does not give true wisdom, for which reverence and respect hold the key (111:10; 112:1); and the God-centred life should be a happy one, not a grudging obedience (112:1).

By contrast, the man who knows in his heart what the service of God means, and yet refuses it, melts away like the snow in summer (112:10).

As in Proverbs, we have in Psalm 112 God's ideal for life in a properly ordered community. As it is, a Christian can earn the respect of his fellows for his standards, and so will prosper. Other psalms show some exceptions, for which God has different answers.

THOUGHT: Consider these psalms in the light of Leviticus 19:2 and Matthew 5:48).

113;114 From poverty to riches

The group of Psalms 113-118 are known as the Hallel, and are sung at the chief festivals of the Jews. At the Passover Psalms 113 and 114 are sung before the meal, following the telling of the Exodus story, and Psalms 115-118 are sung afterwards. It is not known how old this custom is, but some have pictured Jesus and his disciples singing these psalms during the Last Supper (e.g. Matt. 26:30).

Both psalms celebrate the acts of God in bringing the individual (113) and the nation (114) from poverty to riches, from slavery to the free land of God's choice.

Psalm 113 is a completely outgoing hymn of praise to God. It asks for nothing, but glories in his supremacy. There is no contradiction between the Jewish and Christian belief that God in heaven is also active on earth.

There is no idea of the Lord as living in the sky, but the word *above* is used in the sense of *beyond* the universe which he has created (113:4-6). Hence he is Lord of all nations, and not limited to Israel (3, 4). His greatness is shown in a way that the average person would regard as strange. He is concerned to establish those who are looked down upon (7-9; Matt. 11:19). Now the psalmist gives practical expression to this by actually incorporating the words of the barren woman, Hannah, who wrote verses 7, 8 (1 Sam. 2:8). Probably the final Hallelujah belongs to Psalm 114.

The sheer joy of this psalm defies a commentary. It skips for joy at the story of the deliverance from Egypt, with the accompanying miracles of the Red Sea, the earthquake on Sinai, and the rolling back of the Jordan (3-6). Now the Lord from heaven has his centre of action in Judah and Israel, with his sanctuary in Jerusalem (2). One more miracle is selected as a triumphant finale. This is the living water from the rock, which is the miracle with which Paul concludes in 1 Corinthians 10:4. There he points out that the rock was always there when and where it was needed, as though it followed them, as indeed it follows us, for 'the Rock was Christ'. (See also Ps. 110:7.)

THOUGHT: Why is God specially concerned with the downtrodden? Should I be more concerned than I am?

115 Rising above criticism

This psalm was almost certainly composed for corporate singing in the Temple. Among other reasons for coming together for worship there is the need to encourage one another in the faith. We may grow discouraged by the publicity so often given to doubts and criticisms of the faith. 'Where is their God?' (2) is a modern as well as an ancient criticism. If God can be bowed out of the world, that is the end of much moral restraint. We come together to declare, 'Here is our God'.

What is the alternative to God in heaven, living, personal, active, yes, active on earth? (3). Just petty material things that draw the devotion that should belong to God. The New Testament equates covetousness with idolatry (Col. 3:5). Naturally in some countries verses 4-8 must still be taken literally. It may be argued that the idol is intended to draw the mind of the worshipper to the presence of the god whom it represents, but it almost always becomes the actual object of worship.

So the appeal is made to the worshippers in the Temple, the priests of Aaron's line, the Levitical assistants (see 135:20), and the ordinary worshippers (9-11) to turn their eyes from the critics of earth to the God of heaven, and to take his help by faith (12-15).

How has the Lord planned his creation? His undisputed rule is in heaven, and he has made men, women, and children (not dead idols) his representatives on earth (16; Gen. 1:28). He has given them a period of life in which to show his praise in their lives, and it is too late to wait in the hope that they can make up after death for what they have neglected in life. Besides, if this psalm describes praise in the Temple, only the living are present there to join in (17).

Death is not, of course, the end for God's people. What begins in outgoing praise now goes on for evermore (18).

THOUGHT: Why is covetousness equated with idolatry?

116;117 Thank you, Lord

The Bible shows how easy it is to forget to say thank you to God, as the nine lepers forgot in Luke 17:12-19. So it prompts us with psalms of gratitude, as Psalm 100, 'For the thank-offering'. Sometimes the full story of answered prayer may be told to the congregation (14, 18, 19). Sometimes perhaps husband and wife will make a service an occasion of special thanks for something that only they know about. They will not forget the offering (17).

This psalm is primarily a thanksgiving for restoration to health. In the Anglican Prayer Book it is included in a service that was until recently used regularly, but is now rare. This was the mother's thanksgiving for a safe birth, called the Churching of Women, and generally taken privately in church. But this psalm can apply to any recovery and can be adapted for other occasions. Thus verses 5-7 are general, and we are often 'brought low'.

It is curious to find the word *simple* used in verse 6, since it is more commonly used in a bad sense to describe the foolish person who rejects the Lord's way (e.g. Prov. 1:22, 32; 7:7; 14:18), but the root of the word expresses *openness*, and one can be open to the Lord as well as to the permissive standards of the day (NB Prov. 9:4, 16). It is used in a good sense in Proverbs 21:11 of one who is open to learn, as also here and in Psalm 19:7; 119:130. So in the depths we do not close our hearts and blame God, but open up to him to learn and be delivered. If he cannot deliver, my fellow grumblers certainly cannot (10, 11).

It is quite usual to make promises if only God will restore us, but easy to forget them afterwards (14; Eccles. 5:4-6). In verse 13 the RSV, JB, GNB and NIV regard the cup as a thank-offering for salvation, and this may well be correct in the context. The verb is a normal word for *take up* (AV, NEB) and many of us have understood the phrase as a metaphor for drinking from the Lord's cup of blessing (23:5). This was symbolised by the cup at the Last Supper (Matt. 26:27, 28).

Psalm 117 is short but full of meaning. God's love and reliability are not only to be experienced by his chosen people, but their experience should be a witness to all nations of his reality. Somehow we must show by our lives, as well as by our lips, that God's steadfast love and faithfulness are the greatest things in the world to us. So 'you shall be my witnesses' (Acts 1:8).

THOUGHT: Why do I love God (116:1)?

118 High triumph

This psalm was probably written for a festival procession held to celebrate some national deliverance (10-14). At the same time most of the psalm can easily be used in thanksgiving by an individual for something good that he has experienced. Thus it resembles Psalm 116.

Although the representatives of the nation have come together (2-4), it would seem to be the king who leads the procession. In response to prayer (5) and without allies (8, 9) he has beaten off the enemy attack and won the victory in the name of the Lord (10-14).

The procession reaches the gates of the city or possibly the Temple enclosure, and the king ceremonially asks the guards, or the priests, for admission. The response is the opening of the gates for the righteous king (19, 20; as in 24:7-10).

The verses that follow were recognised by Jews and by Jesus as messianic. David, and subsequent kings of his line, foreshadow the final righteous King of Davidic descent. David seemed to be a rejected nobody when he was an outlaw in the later days of Saul's reign, when Saul was trying to build up the nation, but he became the chief cornerstone (22). Now this day (24) celebrates his triumph, and it is commemorated by later kings.

The expression 'Save us' (25) has been transliterated into Greek and English as *Hosanna*. The king is blessed from the Temple (26). It is uncertain what is happening in the last two lines of verse 27, but probably the procession has been carrying leafy branches and is bringing them to surround the altar with its projecting horns at the four corners (Exod. 27:2; 1 Kings 1:50).

We can see how Jesus was identified by himself and others with this King Messiah, when he rode into Jerusalem on Palm Sunday and entered the Temple courts. The people shouted their Hosannas, and blessed him as the Messianic Son of David who came in the name of the Lord (25, 26; Matt. 21:9). They carried branches as they went to meet him, some of which they spread on the road before him (27; John 12:13; Matt. 21:8). He was welcomed in the Temple (26), but not by the priests; their place was taken by children (Matt. 21:15).

When his authority was challenged, Jesus quoted from this psalm, identifying himself with the rejected stone, which became the chief stone of the building (22; Matt. 21:42).

THOUGHT: Trace the picture of the stone, as foundation and top stone, in Isaiah 28:16; Zechariah 3:9; 4:7-10; Acts 4:11; Ephesians 2:20; 1 Peter 2:4-8.

Questions for further study and discussion on Psalms 107–118

1. Are there further categories you would like to see included in Psalm 107 in the light of modern life? Compose a thanksgiving for them.

2. Psalm 109 can be understood as a dialogue, and all the psalms are poems. The Song of Solomon is a drama. The church today has come once more to value literary and artistic talents, though writers and artists can still be misunderstood. What particular difficulties do they face? How can the churches help them to make the fullest use of their gifts?

3. Study the New Testament quotations of Psalm 110:1. In what way do you find these challenging and encouraging?

4. What do we mean when we talk of 'the fear of the Lord' (Ps. 111:10, 112:1)? Why is this the beginning of wisdom? What is meant by wisdom?

5. It has been said that, 'There is an inseparable bond between religion and politics.' What does this mean? Do you agree? If not, why not? If you do, where are Christians failing (compare Ps. 113)?

6. Think of today's idols. How would you mock them in the style of Psalm 115?

7. 'Cursed is the man who trusts in man and makes flesh his arm' (Jer. 17:5; compare Ps. 118:8). Today, rightly, there is emphasis on fellowship and togetherness, but what are the dangers?

Psalm 119 is written in an alphabetic (acrostic) form. The 176 verses are broken into twenty-two groups of eight verses in each. Working in alphabetical order each section takes one letter of the Hebrew twenty-two letter alphabet, and this letter begins each verse in the group. Thus in this section we have the first four letters of the alphabet. The letters do not make any difference to the theme, which is basically the same in each section.

Jesus denounced the scribes and Pharisees of his day for their treatment of Scripture (e.g. Matt. 23:16-22). For many of them Scripture had become a complicated puzzle book, and its exposition was worked out in elaborate ways that were not only a burden (Matt. 23:4) but often ridiculous (Matt. 23:16-22; Mark 7:9-13).

The contents of this psalm show that not all treated God's Word like this, neither when it was written, nor after the exile; neither presumably did teachers like Nicodemus and Gamaliel in the time of Jesus. The Bible as the Word of God was given to be a guide, not a slave driver, for the way of salvation. Notice the wide variety of terms for God's Word. A descriptive noun is used in every verse except verse 122, and it is worth listing them. They represent different aspects of the Word, but are not very different in their significance. We can only seek to share the psalmist's feelings as we read his words quietly.

The psalm opens, as does the entire book of Psalms, with a commendation for those who walk in the way (1), and we ask that our ways may be along God's way (5). We watch for dirty patches (9), and look for signposts (14). We talk to God about our journey (26), and are reassured that God is still our guide along the way (27). When the way forks, we ask to choose the right one (29). We know we are guided faithfully by God's Word (30), and suddenly find that the way is clear enough for us to break into a run.

One outstanding verse is verse 18, which has always been Scripture Union's prayer to be used before reading the daily portion.

THOUGHT: The Bible guides from within as well as providing a map for the way.

119:33–72 Not always easy

No verses here require any special note to make their meaning clear, so once again we may look for a theme. The God-guided way is not always easy, for there are forces at work to turn us aside. Sometimes these are great, sometimes mere pinpricks, though nonetheless irritating. For instance, while God's creation is good, there are vanities, emptinesses, which the New Testament calls the 'world', and which have extraordinarily attractive powers (37). Then again there are the sniping criticisms of our position as Christians which we dread (39, 42, 51). We may well be called to say why we believe as we do, even occasionally in high-up circles (46).

What ought we to feel about unbelievers? Generally we distinguish between the lost sheep and the misleading shepherds (Ezek. 34:1-6). For the former we have sympathy, but with the latter we rightly feel indignant (53) as we find them militant, sneering, or belittling the gospel that God has given us. Sometimes we feel imprisoned in their clever arguments (61). There are answers, and wiser men and women than ourselves have seen them, but, if we cannot see them ourselves, we find strength in knowing that the Bible assures us that it is so.

It is hard when those who dislike us make up lies about us (69). Naturally we try to justify ourselves, not only for our own sake but for the sake of the Lord whom we represent. Yet we must constantly check ourselves to see that our conduct tallies with God's precepts. God's ways are valuable for their own sake, but observing them is all the more vital when we set an example to others.

The Christian life is not easy, although some have a smoother path than others. There are other afflictions beside personal enemies (50), but it is possible to rise all the stronger as a result of meeting them as one who belongs to the Lord (50, 67, 71).

THOUGHT: A bad night is never easy, but it may be put to good use (55, 62).

119:73–112 Your Word a light

In these notes we have assumed that the psalmist is speaking of the Bible when he uses the various descriptive terms of God's Word. If, as is virtually certain, this psalm belongs to a time after the exile, the writer had a reasonable amount of the Old Testament on which to meditate. The Pentateuch, that is, the 'law', was basic and the inspired words of the prophets must have been written down during their lifetime or immediately afterwards, since otherwise they could not have been preserved (Isa. 8:16; Jer. 36:2). There was already a collection of psalms from the time of David onwards. There would have been some access to the historical records, and, if the psalmist was a priest or Levite, he could consult the Temple records which form a large part of the Book of Chronicles. From all these sources the psalmist gathered the precepts, commandments, and words which opened him out to God, and gave him courage to face the attacks that came upon him because he was a believer.

Thus the Word of God is like a light in a dark place (105). It may not be the sun in broad daylight, because much of our pilgrimage is conducted in semi-darkness, when we may be suddenly attacked (85-87), and when we need faith and assurance to keep on when we cannot see into the distance. In fact our range of vision is limited. To blend the GNB and JB in verse 96: 'I have learnt that everything has limits; but your commandment has no limits at all'. So we keep walking in the pool of light towards the unseen horizon.

This does not mean that we are guided into snap decisions by taking random verses from the Bible, but we find that we gradually absorb its wisdom into ourselves. This accounts for the apparently insolent assertion in verses 99, 100. We may simplify it by saying that through God's Word I know more of God than do unbelieving teachers (perhaps the enemies of v. 98 are enemies of God's Word) and old people who have not profited by the study of it. But we may also say that the best of teachings, and the experience of age, must be secondary to the teachings that come from God (Eccles. 12:11, 12). In other words, we must test religious teachings by the light of Scripture.

THOUGHT. The light shows us in our true light as well as lighting our way (Eph. 5:8-14).

119:113–144 Single-minded study

When one speaks of the full inspiration of the Bible, one is often accused of bibliolatry, i.e. worship of the Book rather than of God. Generally those who make this accusation are waiting to slip in some concept of God, Christ, or the work of Christ that contradicts, or goes beyond, what the Bible actually says.

This section again shows how love of the Bible is far from bibliolatry. The Bible is the key that unlocks the knowledge of God and our experience of him. Today people with varied religious experiences are claiming recognition and authority. They may, or may not, have elements of truth, but this must be determined, not by feelings, but by what the Scriptures say. The Scriptures of course include the record of Christ and his teachings, about which we know nothing at all except from the New Testament.

Here the psalmist distils his experience from what God has shown in the Book. This is not bibliolatry.

One thing the Bible student, as this psalmist, realises is the need for faith, since faith lays hold of what is read. If our faith is to be effective, we must first be single-minded, seriously asking what the Lord intends to say. Then we can look for the promise (116) or precepts (128). If a promise applies to our situation, we ask God to help us to realise it by faith in our lives. This may mean a sudden experience, or it may come gradually (123).

A precept also may need faith, because often we cannot keep it in our own strength. It is more than a matter of making up our mind; rather we need to ask for the strength which only God can give (114, 116, 133). The end of everything, as always in this psalm, is the happy awareness that God is God, and yet that he has spoken to us in words that we can understand (130, 144).

Note. Verse 122: this is the only verse in the whole psalm which is without some synonym for the Scriptures. One can only guess at the reason.

THOUGHT: The purpose of single-minded study is summed up in 2 Timothy 3:16, 17 and 2 Peter 1:19-21.

119:145–176 God with us

Although we have come to the end of this long psalm, there is no attempt to sum everything up in a climax, as in many other psalms. The final section is as gently balanced as all the rest. In a sense it is typical of all that we look for in the Scriptures. They challenge us in our time with promises, precepts, and attacks from enemies, but they lift us into the timelessness of God, ever loving, unchanging, and concerned for generation after generation of his people.

One thing that emerges in all the sections is the nearness of God to us. The Bible is not just the record of a nation's history, but it is a history in which God involves himself, and in which he prepares for his own coming in the incarnation of the Messiah. That is why the psalmist can write as he does.

The promises, statutes and precepts are for the moulding of the individuals and of the nation. God truly cares, and the events that I encounter today matter to him. So I dare to declare that he is with me in everything. This is the nucleus of this whole psalm, including these final four sections.

Prayer is talking to God, who is present, and, if we begin the day by opening up to him (147, 148), we shall continue it with the frequent recollection of his presence (151). A brief prayer of praise or thanks is never out of place (164).

Much of the psalm is outgoing. This means that, while there are certainly petitions for help (149, 153), we are continually drawn out in praise and thanksgiving for all that we know of God through his Word and in the experience that his Word has enabled us to have (162, 171, 172).

Perhaps after all there is a climax at the very end. In the psalm the psalmist has repeatedly spoken of his zeal and his longing for God. Is he then a super-believer? He often seems far beyond us, and certainly he sets a pattern for us to follow. Yet, after all, like ourselves he began as a lost sheep, and still needs the shepherd's care (176).

THOUGHT: The psalmist finds so much in God's Word, yet how much more there is for Christians!

120 From the City of Destruction

We have been travelling through a pleasant landscape in Psalm 119 with a similarity of scenery. If we were only dipping into the Scriptures, it would probably be best to take a single section quietly by itself. Now the compiler has added a group of psalms that are the very opposite, since they jump from theme to theme, supplying thoughts to occupy a Pilgrim's Progress from the city of destruction to the Celestial City.

In fact their title, A Song of Ascents, is usually taken nowadays to mean a song for pilgrims on their way up to Jerusalem to enjoy one of the three festivals which the people were expected to attend during the year (Deut. 16:16). These psalms were not all written specially for the pilgrimage, although one or two may have been, but probably they were gathered together to form a small collection of suitable hymns.

Psalm 120 forms a good introduction. The pilgrim looks back to the old life, and remembers the 'world' he has left behind him. He left it because he saw it in all its horror, and cried to God to make it possible for him to go (1, 2). He sees the world as primarily a place of lying and deceit, and this is also a New Testament assessment (e.g. John 8:44; Rom. 16:18; Rev. 12:9; 20:3; 22:15). Like Bunyan's Pilgrim, he knows that the false world of lies is doomed to destruction. The tongues that shot down the truth will themselves be pierced with the arrows of truth, and God's fire will consume them (3, 4).

The pilgrim had lived there all too long, and it sounds as though his town was largely pagan. He names Meshech and Kedar as typical pagan places. He cannot have been living in both of them, since Meshech is near the Black Sea and Kedar is in Arabia. The GNB and JB paraphrase in somewhat similar words; 'Living among you is as bad as living in Meshech, or camping in Kedar.'

The other mark of the world is disturbance. Sadly, we must still take this literally. One may also draw out the spiritual meaning here. Peace of soul can come only from God, but the simple gospel of peace still rouses antagonism (6, 7).

Note. Ascents can mean steps, and a Jewish tradition was that these 15 psalms were sung by Levites on the 15 steps between two of the Temple courts. This would not rule them out as pilgrim psalms.

THOUGHT: What do I expect to find on my pilgrimage?

121;122 Help by the way

What a change from the violence of the previous psalm! Now it is all 'the LORD' (2, 5, 7, 8). The pilgrim, like Bunyan's Christian, has a sight of the Delectable Mountains (1) in place of the Hill called Error found in Psalm 120. These mountains 'belong to the Lord', and from there he sends his help. The great Creator is ready to help needy pilgrims (2). He is the perfect Guide, unsleeping (3, 4), watching for danger (5), able to break the burning heat of the sun and the intense, disturbing glare of the full moon (6).

The promise in verse 7a reminds us of the Lord's Prayer, 'Deliver us from evil'. In previous notes (e.g. Ps. 91) we have realised that there may be times when Christians suffer as do non-Christians, but as pilgrims we are right to step out each day confident that all will be well (7b). The Christian life would indeed be impossible if we could not look for the guided life (8).

Notes. Verses 1, 2. The alternative interpretation is that it is useless to look for help to the hills where heathen gods are worshipped. But see 125:2.

Psalm 122 anticipates the purpose of the journey to the Celestial City, which is to meet with the Lord in his temple (1, 2). According to the title the psalm comes from a Davidic collection. David intended Jerusalem to be the centre which would draw the nation together, as God had planned through Moses (4; Deut. 12:5, 6). It would be the throne of the kings of David's line, ancestors of the Messiah (5; Deut. 17:15), who is the Prince of Peace (Isa. 9:6), the peace the pilgrim hoped to find (6-8).

We may translate this into down-to-earth Christian experience. We speak of coming together in God's house (1). We should be in fellowship and at peace with one another, since God's pilgrims are not isolated individuals (4, 8). We may also see in this pilgrim psalm 'the city which has foundations' (Heb. 11:10), 'the heavenly Jerusalem' (Heb. 12:22), where the Prince of Peace is the eternal King, and where in him the whole body finds peace for ever (Eph. 2:14-17).

THOUGHT: What makes the journey worthwhile? How would you encourage someone who felt like giving up?

Questions for further study and discussion on Psalms 119–122

1. Study the words used in Psalm 119 for the Scriptures. What light do they throw on the nature and purpose of God's Word?

2. H. L. Ellison writes, 'The Law was intended to cover all possibilities of life, hence man needed divine wisdom to infer God's will for those eventualities not directly covered by it (119:12). He was not merely a learner but also a teacher (13).' Do you believe this is true for the Christian today?

3. What controversial issues today are not mentioned in the Bible? What principles do we follow as we try to understand the Christian view of these issues?

4. Choose one such issue and discuss the questions a Christian should be asking about it.

5. How would you define 'the inspiration of the Bible'?

6. Discuss your favourite verse from Psalm 119.

7. Express in modern terms your understanding of the meaning of pilgrimage for the Christian.

8. 'He's so heavenly minded he's no earthly use.' How would you answer such a jibe?

123;124 Help from above

The Psalms, and indeed the whole Bible, speak of God as present everywhere (e.g. 139:7-12), and yet know that he is 'centred' above (123:1). Critics represent this as a difficulty, using the slogan that what is up in Britain is down in Australia. But *up* is *away* in any part of the world, and heaven is away from earth, as we are reminded every time we pray the Lord's Prayer: 'Thy kingdom come, Thy will be done, on earth as it is in heaven.'

It is impossible for us to visualise heaven. The most we can say is that it is a sphere or dimension where God is loved, praised, and obeyed absolutely. Inasmuch as this sphere is not on earth, we are bound to look up to 'our Father who art in heaven'. So not only the pilgrim psalmist (123:1) but Jesus Christ (John 11:41; 17:1), and the New Testament Christians (1 Tim. 2:8), looked up when they prayed.

So the pilgrim is like the man in the picture in Bunyan's Interpreter's House, who had 'eyes lifted up to heaven'. Like a good servant he (or she) looks to see what the master or mistress requires, and knows that the needed protection will be given (2).

The pilgrim looks back to the scorn with which he was treated by those who made themselves comfortable in the world, not heaven (3, 4), and goes on to sing, in Psalm 124, another psalm of David that continues this theme. David had many battles during his reign, and he celebrates a victory in a war that would have disintegrated the nation. Where would the pilgrim have been then?

As generation after generation of pilgrims came, each would remember the last threat to the nation. Some threats were deserved, as the prophets showed, but again and again God gave deliverance (e.g. 2 Kings 19:35, 36; Pss. 46 and 48). No doubt also pilgrims who had not passed through a national crisis could look back to deliverance from personal attacks. So today, while we give thanks for national deliverance, many also have, or have had, their private struggles in factory, shop, place of business, in the neighbourhood, or even in the home. Psalm 123 is their prayer for deliverance, while Psalm 124 gives thanks for deliverance that has come.

THOUGHT: Psalm 124:8 is a magnificent text for the day.

125;126 The happy land

Psalm 125 tells of God's people in the happy land that he has given to them. Zion ringed by mountains is a picture of her inhabitants ringed by the Lord (2). They are linked to him, as we are, by the lifeline of faith (1).

A problem can arise if the predominant climate is temptingly evil. Sadly enough the sceptre (or power) of wickedness (3) is ever ready to dominate the people of the land, both materially, intellectually, and spiritually, and even Christians can give way. NEB speaks of the sceptre 'finding a home' in the land. We must be alert to this threat and take every opportunity that comes to prevent wholesale contamination.

This means we must make clear the difference between good and evil. The good look to God for encouragement (4), and avoid the slippery path to destruction (5). So Bunyan closes his first book, 'Then I saw that there was a way to hell, even from the gates of heaven, as well as from the City of Destruction.'

Psalm 126 describes the happiness of restoration after loss, whether or not the loss was deserved, as the prophets so often show, or apparently undeserved. Jealous nations, who once may have been God's instruments in punishment, now see that God's hand has been at work (e.g. Neh. 6:16).

The first half of the psalm celebrates what God has done in the past. Verses 4-6 are for the pilgrim who comes from an oppressed or depressed community. He has travelled through dry places, like those in the south, but has seen the dry watercourses filled again by the winter rains, so that the frustrated sowers can at last look for a crop. He prays for such an experience for Zion and himself.

THOUGHT: Psalm 126:5, 6 is often applied to winning souls for Christ. Is this useful? See also John 4:35, 36.

127;128 The family

It is natural for the pilgrim to sing psalms by David and Solomon as he travels to the city where these were the first two great kings. In the first two verses of Psalm 127 Solomon has in mind the capital city that he built when he came to the throne, and obviously he includes the Temple and other buildings (1 Kings 7). At that time he was sincerely devoted to God, as his prayer in 1 Kings 8:20, 27 shows, and he knew that God was with him in his work (1).

What was true of his large scale work is of course true of all building, and indeed of all work. Whether our labour be mental or physical it is easy to overdo it by working all hours of the day and night (2). So we wear ourselves out. Solomon evidently knew the benefits of relaxation, and perhaps even of God's use of the mind-below-the-surface when we sleep (2b).

There are two possible translations of the last line of verse 2, both true. The AV and RV, 'he gives to his beloved sleep', is recognised by the RSV margin and NIV. This makes good sense. Instead of becoming so burdened that we suffer from insomnia, let us look for a quiet confidence in God so that sleep refreshes us. If he is behind our building, we can relax. Most modern translations prefer, 'he gives to his beloved in sleep'. This can mean that God, as it were, goes on working when we have to stop, showing that the work is his. Or, in modern terms, he works in the subconscious to refit us for what we have to do.

Next Solomon praises the ideal family, where children and parents unite to give the family strength against the outside world. 'The gate' (5) was the equivalent of the law court, but it was naturally the place of informal argument as well (Job 29:7). Presumably Solomon wrote this when he was young (4). It is curious that in spite of his many wives (1 Kings 11:3) only one of his sons, Rehoboam, is mentioned in the history.

In Psalm 128 the pilgrim is encouraged to look for a happy family life, which includes satisfying work so that he can support his wife and children (2). One of the great sadnesses of modern industrial society is that so few can 'eat the fruit of your own labours' (NEB). It may be that constructive hobbies are the only solution in such cases.

A good mother and vigorous children make the home (3), and it is possible that 'within your house' (3), or 'in the innermost parts of thine house' (RV), indicates that the house is large enough for the wife to have her own room. A happy family needs a happy city (5) with no wars to slaughter children and grandchildren (6).

THOUGHT: The change of social conditions, when large families are difficult, change the literal application of the psalm. What permanent elements can be retained?

129;130 In the depths

It is impossible for each psalm to reflect every mood and experience of the pilgrim, but he probably finds some answering chord in each one. Here is the humiliation of being a member of a nation that is despised and has often been violently attacked (1, 2). Israel's enemies yoked them, as it were, to the plough and lashed them with whips (3). But the Lord cut the rope that tied them and let them go free (4; Job 39:10).

It is important to note that these enemies are motivated by hate, and Israel is not being punished, as is suggested in the next psalm. So it is proper to pray that they may be turned back (5), and wither like the grass that seeds itself on the roof. Passers-by greet the reapers in the field but no one wishes these enemies well (8; Ruth 2:4).

Psalm 130 also sounds a note of tragedy, but now the pilgrim searches his heart to see whether his suffering is deserved. He does not name 'the depths' into which he, a sinner, has sunk. They may describe some savage illness, persecution, or intense mental depression. Just as Paul does not say what form his 'thorn in the flesh' took (2 Cor. 12:7), so the psalmist leaves his suffering undescribed so that we may identify our own 'depths' with the thought of the psalm.

If the depths are traceable to sin, the first need is forgiveness. Then we can once more come before the Lord, not dismissing our sin lightly but standing in awe (GNB) of the One who so wonderfully forgives (3, 4).

While forgiveness is immediate, the full deliverance for which we hope may not come instantly (5, 6). The thought of waiting for the Lord comes in other places in Scripture, e.g. Psalms 37:34; 40:1; Isaiah 25:9; Hosea 12:6; Romans 8:23, 25. The repetition of the sentence about the watchmen suggests the constant watching for the dawn, and perhaps calling the hours of the night (6; see also the repetition in Isa. 21:11, 12).

Israel's confidence, and ours, lies in the Lord who delights to show his steadfast love (7). Once again the pilgrim gladly accepts God's total forgiveness (8).

THOUGHT: What does waiting on the Lord mean to me today?

131;132 Rest and activity

A biography or autobiography of someone much in the public eye will often give a surprising revelation of some simplicities in the life pattern. From the history one would judge David to be a highly active man of war, but Psalm 131, perhaps written in old age, shows him in a different light. He had learned to live within his capacity, and he did not pry into theological theories outside God's revelation (1; Deut. 29:29; 30:11-14). Would that we all knew more of this restfulness, which might percolate from us to others around (3).

Yet rest must be coupled with activity, and Psalm 132 gives an equally striking picture of David in action when the situation demanded it. What a picture of enthusiasm for the Lord is given in verses 2-5! The psalm is the eyewitness account of how David was moved to bring the ark from Kiriath-jearim (8 miles WNW of Jerusalem, and also called Baale-judah in 2 Sam. 6:2) where it had been taken after the Philistines returned it (6; 1 Sam. 7:1, 2). Even the exact whereabouts of the ark had been forgotten (6). The twenty years of 1 Samuel 7:2 represent the period to the time when Samuel took charge of the nation (1 Sam. 7:3). Actually some seventy years elapsed from the ark's capture to the day when David brought it in triumph to Jerusalem (2 Sam. 6).

Since the words of verses 8-10 are similar to the concluding words of Solomon's dedicatory prayer in 2 Chronicles 6:41, 42, it may be that he is the author of the psalm, and that he is relating what David and others had told him. Thus the vow of verses 2-5 is not recorded elsewhere. Certainly the reminder of God's promise to David of the son upon his throne would come well from Solomon (11; 89:3, 4).

God's presence was mysteriously concentrated in the holy of holies in the Temple, and especially around the ark (7, 8; 1 Kings 8:6-11). One might use the analogy of the sun's rays focused in a bright and burning spot through the lens of a magnifying glass (13, 14). God wished to satisfy his people (15), and to forge a spiritual link with himself (16). Ultimately his purposes were to come to a climax in the Son of David who would arise as the strong horn and the shining light (17; Luke 1:69, 79). That light would show all his enemies in their true colour, when they saw him as the King of kings (18).

THOUGHT: There are occasions when David's zeal in Psalm 132:3-5 is a challenge to us.

133;134 In unity

The pilgrim is coming to the end of his hymn book. The days spent in close contact with his travelling companions, and with the crowds in the Temple, may well have brought tensions which might induce him to withdraw into himself. This is not God's way, since Jerusalem is the place of coming together (1, 122:3, 4). Yet church history is littered with splintered groups of Christians. And even in our smaller communities we tend to allow natural quarrelsomeness to spill over into Christian relationships.

The simile of the oil is strange to us, although it was meaningful to the Jews. The original reference is to Exodus 29:5-7, but probably the psalmist had seen one of Aaron's descendants anointed as Aaron was. The simile of the dew is easier, although the meaning is generally taken to be that Zion is refreshed by dew that is as heavy as that which falls on Hermon. Dewy mist does not drift the two hundred miles between the two places.

We do not know anything about night services in the Temple (134:1), but 1 Chronicles 9:33 speaks of certain Levites who sang in the Temple during the night as well as the day. Earnest pilgrims, with only a limited time to spare, would doubtless spend some of the quiet night worshipping with the Temple singers.

As the closing psalm in the hymn book of Ascents, this is a reminder that, although the pilgrims go back to their homes, they are in unity with the worship of God that continues in Jerusalem, uninterrupted even by the close of day. Pilgrim and Levite are together in the unity of blessing and being blessed (2, 3). One thinks of the hymn, 'The day Thou gavest, Lord, is ended . . .' which reads:

We thank Thee that Thy Church unsleeping,
While earth rolls onward into light,
Through all the world her watch is keeping,
And rests not now by day or night.

THOUGHT: Is there anyone with whom I am not 'in unity'? How can I put things right?

Questions for further study and discussion on Psalms 123–134

1. The pilgrim collection is rich in word pictures. Make a list of them and consider what modern equivalents could be suggested.

2. How do you explain the differing attitudes to prosperity in the Old and New Testaments?

3. How does Psalm 126:6 challenge the Christian work we do? What encouragement is there in it?

4. What circumstances today should guide Christians over the size of their family?

5. Many businessmen today have turned into 'workaholics', able to do nothing but work (compare 127:2). How would you counsel such people?

6. Has the same thing happened to some Christian leaders and workers? What are the symptoms? What is the cause and the cure?

7. What may have led David to write as he did in Psalm 131? What do you find most challenging about this Psalm? What New Testament parallels are there to the thoughts here?

8. What are the main virtues inculcated by the pilgrim collection?

9. What implications does Psalm 133 have for church unity?

135 An anthology of quotations

This psalm is largely a succession of quotations or reminiscences of earlier Scriptures. It is a reminder that a well-stored mind can build up helpful prayers based on the Bible. The editor has presumably placed it here because of its opening links with the previous psalm. The Lord's goodness and graciousness are the subject of special praise in the Temple (3; 147:1), and are here demonstrated in various ways. First, God has chosen Israel as his own (4; Deut. 7:6). Secondly, unlike the nature gods (5), he is the Creator and Upholder of the whole natural order (6; 115:3; Exod. 20:4), and is the God of the rain and storm (7; Jer. 10:13; see also note on Ps. 29). Next, he has shown his concern for the people of Israel by bringing them out of Egypt into Canaan (8-12). Verses 10-12 are repeated in Psalm 136:18-22, and are drawn from the highlights of history. God's past care is a foretaste of present and future mercies (v. 13: Exod. 3:15; v. 14: Deut. 32:36).

The psalmist has already spoken briefly of the aboveness of God over so-called gods (5). Now (15-18) he quotes from Psalm 115:4-8 with very slight variations: here, for example, the voices come on the breath through the mouth; there the sound is formed in the voice-box. He reasserts that a person becomes like the god he or she worships (18). This was particularly true of Canaanites, whose pantheon was especially degrading.

The psalm ends, as it began, with a call to worship. The Temple servants are now specified, and the ordinary worshippers join them (19, 20; 115:9-11; 118:2-4). The closing verse centres the Lord in Zion, although previously he is visualised as above (5-7). This is characteristic of the psalms, and corresponds to Christian experience. God is in heaven, and yet by his Spirit he is present in his temple on earth (1 Cor. 3:16; Eph. 2:21, 22).

THOUGHT: If covetousness is idolatry (Eph. 5:5), have I an idol which is moulding me (18)?

136 A song of steadfast love

Obviously this psalm was composed for responsive singing. Probably the leader recited the descriptive line, and the choir and congregation responded with the refrain. It is used today at the Passover, when the head of the family leads and the family respond.

It closely resembles Psalm 135, but contains quotations of its own. Thus it has the same opening as Psalms 106, 107, 118. God's titles (2, 3) come from Deuteronomy 10:17. The features of creation are drawn from Genesis 1. The outline of history (10-22) amplifies Psalm 135:8-12.

The conclusion differs from that of the previous psalm, and is not a quotation from any other Scripture. The verses recognise that the triumphs of history have recently been counterbalanced by a 'low estate'. No details are given, but one notes the explanation in Psalm 106, which, as we have seen, has the same opening as this psalm. Yet God has given deliverance from the foes that have attacked Israel.

So much for Israel, but the psalm closes with the reminder that God cares for 'all flesh' (25), and is rounded off with similar lines to those with which it began. Appropriately God's title in verse 26 is no longer the covenant name, Yahweh, but is 'the God of heaven' (Ezra 1:2).

At the age of fifteen Milton turned this psalm into a Christian hymn, 'Let us with a gladsome mind . . .'. However, a Christian may find it difficult to give thanks for the destruction of Sihon, king of the Amorites. In fact Sihon, and probably Og, refused to allow Israel to pass peacefully through his land, and brought out his army against them (Num. 21:21-24, 33, 34). Pharaoh also had the opportunity to let the people go before the plagues fell on the land (10-15; Exod. 5:1-9).

The joy over other battles and the occupation of Canaan (17, 18, 21, 22) raises further difficulties in our minds. What we can say is that the history of insignificant Israel took a certain course, which, as it culminated in the Messiah, is rightly seen as God-guided through periods when war was accepted as normal. For this the psalmist gives thanks (26).

THOUGHT: 'His steadfast love endures *for ever*' (2, 25).

137 Sacred and secular

Although some commentaries date this psalm after the return from exile because of the past tenses in verses 1-3, it seems from verse 8 that Babylon has not yet been captured by the Persians. So the people had not yet returned. The past tenses make sense if the psalmist is writing after some Jewish festival.

The Lord's songs were still sung among the faithful in exile who kept the festivals as best they could, but the songs were out of place for happy singing in public. They were certainly not to be sung for the entertainment of an unsympathetic, mocking audience. Those who had known Jerusalem before the captivity naturally carried unforgettable memories (5, 6). Even children born in Babylon probably imbibed their parents' memories. One day they knew they would return home. In 605 BC Jeremiah had said that Babylonian domination would last for seventy years (Jer. 25), and that at the end of this period God would bring them back again.

The psalm closes with prayers directed against Edom and Babylon. There is no indication that Babylon persecuted the Jews in exile, unless they broke the law (Jer. 29:21-32), and the reference is clearly to their extreme behaviour at the taking of Jerusalem. The Babylonians had done their best to destroy the city totally (2 Kings 25:9, 10), while Edom encouraged them (Obad. 10-14).

History shows that brutality breeds brutality, and one oppressive kingdom goes down before another (Rev. 13:10). But what are we to say about the prayers in verses 7-9? Both were answered in general, but not as the psalmist expected. Edom eventually lost its identity as it was absorbed into Judah. The second prayer for the brutal murder of Babylonian babies (9), in retaliation for the murder of the Jewish babies at the fall of Jerusalem, has shocked most consciences. The writer of these notes does not wish to be irreverent, but it seems to him that God allowed this prayer in order to shock readers into serious thought, and then answered the prayer in a strange way. Babylon was probably the only city of antiquity in which this murder of babies did not happen when it was captured. Both Babylonian and Persian records say that Cyrus of Persia entered Babylon without a battle, so that Babylon suffered no harm.

THOUGHT: From time to time Christian and Jewish hymns, including this psalm, are turned into 'pop'. Is this the Lord's song in a strange land?

138 The King and the kings

Psalm 138 was written after David had brought the ark to Jerusalem and set up a tabernacle for it. The word 'temple' (2) may well have been substituted for whatever word David used to describe his temporary structure (so also 5:7).

His many campaigns had made him think of God's ultimate purpose for the throne of David. As we have seen, he had been made aware of the Messiah who would come from his line (e.g. Psalms 2 and 110). Would he be a great conqueror? In one sense, yes, but he would not be a violent dictator (6). He would be an interpreter of God's message to the kings of the earth (4), and lead them also to praise the true God (5). Of this God David had no doubts. The nations had their gods (1), but in the end they must surely come to the living God.

How different Jehovah is from the so-called gods of the nations, with his steadfast love and faithfulness and the majesty of his reputation (name) and his revelation (2). Alternatively, following the literal Hebrew (as RSV margin), God's promise (word) is even greater than we have been told, i.e. more than we can imagine (JB; Eph. 3:20). Answered prayer means added inner strength (3), and past and present deliverance gives full assurance for the future. This is not haphazard but has God's purpose in it.

Note. The conversion of the kings (4) may indicate the spread of the gospel through many countries and states. Symbolising this was the tradition that the three magi were three kings (Matt. 2:1; Isa. 60:3). Those who believe in an earthly millennium see that as the time of fulfilment. Whatever the period, there is an obvious link with the thought of Isaiah 60 and Revelation 21:24.

THOUGHT: Our faith is for others to share.

139 God ever present

David is lost in wonder at the thought of God's omnipresence and omniscience. God has total knowledge of him, even more than David has of himself (1-6; 1 Cor. 13:12). Moreover it is impossible to move out of the orbit of God's presence, although this is not to say that everyone has fellowship with God. Some say that the writer of verses 7-12 had been trying to avoid God, but this interpretation does not tally with what we know of David, nor with the whole context of the psalm, especially of verse 10. The passage is more likely to be a happy assurance of God's presence in every circumstance, even in the unknown sphere of the departed. In verse 11 it may be preferable to emphasise fear rather than desire to escape by following the NEB, 'If I say, Surely darkness will steal over me, night will close around me . . . .'

The verses that follow, describing conception and growth in the womb, are among the most beautiful in literature. The writer of these notes heard them read effectively at the funeral of an elderly doctor who had brought many children into the world. It is sad if we have to sacrifice the AV and RV rendering, 'I am fearfully and wonderfully made', but the RSV margin shows the difficulty of translation without amending the text. It is, however, retained by the NIV, and in another form by the JB, 'For the wonder of myself, for the wonder of your works'.

The darkness of the womb is compared to a cave in verse 15, and this is also the meaning in Ephesians 4:9 which refers to the genuinely human conception and incarnation of the pre-existent Christ. The development of the unformed foetus is pictured in verse 16, when, as it were, the parts of the body were all laid down according to God's map of human anatomy. It is not necessary to interpret the passage of predestination, although this is possible. It depends on whether the writing refers to the foreseen days of life (RSV, GNB, JB, NIV), or to the parts of the body, as suggested above. So NEB, '. . . and in thy book they are all recorded; day by day they were fashioned, not one of them was late in growing.'

The closing verses (19-24) may at first sight appear to introduce a theme which does not belong to the rest of the psalm, but good and evil are never far from the Jewish mind. The significant thing is that David does not admit one law for the obviously wicked and another for himself. He takes God's side in the struggle against evil, but his jealousy for God demands that he digs deeply into himself in case he also is, after all, one of the wicked whom God must judge and destroy.

THOUGHT: Ecclesiastes 11:5; John 3:8 (margins as a possibility).

140 Evil must be turned back

Psalms 140-143 bring us once more to David's confrontation with his enemies, who, because of their whole outlook, were also the enemies of God. The editor may have included those psalms here because of the ending of Psalm 139. The heading of Psalm 142 associates it with David's outlaw period, and it could be that Psalm 140 was also written then.

The enemies are described in poetical terms as those who are determined to catch David by one means or another. Their poisonous words inflame Saul in case he shows signs of weakening (2, 3; 1 Sam. 24:16-22). It is natural that there was such intense hostility to David. Today there are similar clashes of feeling when a revolution is brewing in some country and the supporters of the establishment are in bitter conflict with the revolutionaries.

David is not a revolutionary, but Saul is treating him as such, and it is important for men at the top to be on the right side, that is, the side that will ultimately win (1 Sam. 22:7, 8). Just now Saul is a dangerous man to cross (1 Sam. 22:17-19).

David, as always, turns everything back on God (4). If his enemies try to trap him (4, 5), then they in their turn must fear God's trap (10). If their tongues spit out poison (3), the poison will infect them (9). Violence (1, 4) will release a shower of burning coals on their heads (10). Those who hunt their prey with vicious slanders will themselves be the victims of the chase (11).

At the moment David is in the weaker position, since he has determined not to retaliate against Saul (1 Sam. 24:10). As always in his life, he finds protection in the God whom he knows (6-8). God is on the side of those who cannot defend themselves (12) and who try to live after his pattern (13).

THOUGHT: The tongue reveals the heart (2, 3; Luke 6:45).

141 Crime and punishment

This psalm was probably written after David had come to the throne and had brought the ark into Jerusalem. Although he had not built the Temple, he had made a tent to contain the ark (2 Sam. 7:2), and here incense and daily sacrifices were offered (2; 1 Chron. 16:37-40). Perhaps David used to attend in the evening (2), but whenever he prayed he knew that God received his prayer as surely as he received the worship in the sanctuary (2).

As in his outlaw days, David knows the connection between heart and lips (3, 4; 140:2, 3). Even the king is not immune to bribery – not money but, say, invitations to lavish suppers, where too much drink can affect a person's judgement (4).

Better to be corrected by a good man in kindness (a proper use of the tongue) than to have the oily flattery of the tempter (5). The law may well catch up with these tempters, and God's standards will be upheld by the court (6). They are like rocks that damage the plough and have to be broken to pieces; their fate may well be the death sentence (7).

David, as king, has control of the law courts, and it is likely that this is what is in his mind. He is not so much praying here and in Psalm 140 for God's vengeance on his enemies, as looking for the law to deal adequately with crime. The law of 'an eye for an eye and a tooth for a tooth' is still the law of all genuine courts of justice. The judge's sentence includes equivalent compensation for the victim (e.g. the price of his eye) and imprisonment or other punishment for the guilty. So David asserts that the doer of the crime must suffer the equivalent punishment.

Note. The Hebrew of verses 5-7 is difficult. The RSV, NEB, GNB, JB more or less agree on verse 5., but the NIV gives another possibility 'Let a righteous man strike me – it is a kindness; let him rebuke me – it is oil on my head. My head will not refuse it.'

THOUGHT: What encouragement from our prayer-lives can we draw from the parallel with incense in verse 2? What is the significance of prayer as this psalm sees it?

Questions for further study and discussion on Psalms 135–141

1. Try writing a Christian poem along the lines of Psalm 136.

2. Give examples of mockery of Christians today. Suggest positive ways in which we may respond to this.

3. What do you find particularly alien about the world (compare Ps. 137)? Why is it that we rarely sit down and weep? Would our witness in the world be better or worse if we did?

4. To what do you ascribe our frequent hesitation to speak of what God has done for us, materially as well as spiritually? In what ways could the local church be encouraged to overcome it?

5. Each member of your group could play a record, sing or quote a hymn or song, show a picture or photograph, share a poem or verse or experience that for them expresses something of the worship and love of Psalm 139.

6. Should unborn babies be aborted? Discuss this in the light of Psalm 139.

7. Discuss the good and bad use of the tongue, as seen in these Psalms and in James 3:1-12.

8. In Psalm 141 what did David pray to be guarded from? What are some modern equivalents to the pagan meals? What is the difference between this, and Jesus' eating with tax collectors and sinners?

142 Does anyone care?

The heading is similar to that of Psalm 57. There are two occasions recorded when David was in a cave, namely in Adullam (1 Sam. 22:1, 2; 2 Sam. 23:13, 14), and in Engedi, when he spared Saul's life (1 Sam. 24:3). Although some refer this psalm to Engedi, it would seem that this was a very temporary shelter, whereas Adullam was the cave especially connected with David's place of refuge.

This psalm would then belong to David's early days in the cave, since verse 4 complains that he has virtually no supporters. One answer to his prayer was the increased support that he received once it was known that he had settled there (1 Sam. 22: 1, 2).

Meanwhile Adullam was like a prison (7), since Saul's men were scouring the country, and David could not trust the local people (4; 1 Sam. 23:12, 19, 20). So the psalm tells of enmity and treachery, and, as on other occasions, David pours out his heart to God. The language of verse 1 shows that he prayed aloud, and it is likely that vocal prayer was far more frequent then than it is today, for normally most of us pray in silence when we are alone (Luke 18:11, 13; John 17). If we are troubled by too many wandering thoughts in our prayer time, it is helpful to cry with our voice to the Lord (1).

Another hindrance in prayer, beside wandering thoughts, is the feeling that prayer is all in vain, and that our circumstances are too complicated for God to handle. There were times when David's spirit was faint, but, in spite of his feelings, he did not allow them to disturb his faith in God; he knew that God knew and could deliver (3a).

We noticed that one answer to David's prayer was the way in which 400 supporters rallied to his side (1 Sam. 22:2). Yet David had prayed for the support of the righteous (7), while those who actually came were running away from their creditors and were discontented (1 Sam. 22:2). However, David made them into a force to be reckoned with, and one likes to think that he instilled some moral fibre into them.

THOUGHT: Praying aloud may help our concentration.

143 Teach me

The Greek Septuagint translation adds to the heading, '. . . when his son persecuted him', the reference being to Absalom's rebellion. We generally try to interpret a psalm in its setting, and this is as good a background as any. Certainly verse 5 suggests that the psalm belongs to the latter part of David's life. When he fled from Absalom he was wondering whether he was indeed guilty in some way (2; 2 Sam. 16:10). Verse 3 sounds exaggerated but this is the language of poetry.

In verse 6 his appeal for vindication, in reaching beyond man to God, is similar to that in 2 Samuel 16:12. It is even possible that verse 8 is to be taken literally, since David was threatened by a possible night attack (2 Sam. 17:1, 2). His prayer was for a safe night and fresh guidance in the morning. If God is not with him, the darkness of depression (3) will give place to the darkness of actual death (7).

He prays for victory in the coming battle (11, 12), even though this would mean the destruction of many of his adversaries. We know from the history that David still hoped that Absalom could be spared (2 Sam. 18:5), but then he would no longer be an effective adversary.

It may sound absurd to picture David sitting down on this first night to compose a psalm, but his mind exuded poetry, and in modern times too there have been poems from the battlefield, especially during the first World War. And, after all, this psalm is not a poem for publication, but forms David's prayer on that first night of escape.

Whether or not this is the occasion of the psalm, it is a useful prayer when we examine ourselves before God. The RSV on verse 2 gives cross-references to Romans 3:20 and Galatians 2:16, both of which reject self-justification and show the need for God's justification of us through faith in Jesus Christ as our Saviour. Our enemies may be men or women, or they may be strong temptations that threaten to crush us. Sometimes our whole mind dwells on them, but this psalm encourages us to look up to God for victory and for positive guidance by his Holy Spirit.

THOUGHT: There is a saying which runs something like this: 'For every look at self take ten looks at God.'

144 A happy country

Here is David realising his responsibility as king. It is in this light that we must understand verses 1 and 2. The king is responsible for the defence of his country, and David thanks God for the ability that he had given him as leader in battle. At that time war was taken for granted, and God's guidance was given within that framework, but God always held up the ideal of peace as his ultimate desire (1 Chron. 22:8; Isa. 9:7; and almost every reference to the Messiah). It was many centuries before nations were prepared to band together to exchange war for negotiations, and even now we walk on a knife-edge.

If David thanks God for the ability to fulfil his position, we may thank him for the ability he has given us for our calling, whether it is the ability to work the coal face; to handle accounts; to care for the sick as doctor, nurse, or orderly, to serve behind the counter; to serve as policeman or in the fire service; or to be a mother and housewife, or anything else.

David knows his weakness as a mere human (3, 4), but in vivid poetry he sees his great God as coming down in power to rescue him, and consequently his country, from the false standards of alien paganism (5-8). These standards are sufficiently important for David to mention them again (11), but this time he visualises more than infiltration. Defeat in battle could involve the destruction of the city and consequently of the God-given Jewish way of life. Immigrants have ways of behaviour that we find strange, but these cultural differences are not what David objects to. In fact he had foreigners in his service (2 Sam. 15:19, 22), and presumably they tended to accept his standards.

So he comes to the ideal towards which he had tried to guide the community. Freedom and peace would allow boys and girls to grow to maturity (12; Zech. 8:5). Agriculture would flourish without enemies descending to rob the crops (13; Judges 6:3-5), and rich pastures would support large flocks of sheep and herds of cattle (13, 14). Then nobody would cry out in need (14b). Here is David's picture of a happy and peaceful state. War may be necessary but this state must be held in mind as God's ideal (15).

Note. Although some commentaries say that the material in this psalm is taken from other psalms, this can be misleading. It is not a scrapbook of collected verses, but phrases that had lingered in David's mind, especially from Psalm 18 (compare, for example, v. 1 and 18:34; v. 5 and 18:9; v. 9 and 33:2; v. 10 and 18:50.

THOUGHT: Can we adapt verses 12-15 to the needs of our country today?

145 Outburst of praise

This is the last of the alphabetic (acrostic) psalms. The initial letter of each verse follows the order of the Hebrew alphabet. In the standard Hebrew text the letter N is missing, but the modern translations that we have been using all supply the N verse as 13b or 14a, using other manuscripts (see margin). God has preserved the text of the Scriptures in a remarkable way down the centuries, but belief in the full inspiration of the Bible 'as originally given' allows for errors in copying before the fixture of printing. None of these variations affects any vital doctrine, and scholars who specialise in the text are able to make constructive suggestions for the best reading.

Although some commentators speak of the connection of thought as loose, because of the alphabetic scheme, the paragraphs of the RSV indicate some division of themes. There is no reason why the need to use one special letter at the beginning of each verse should hamper the expression of thought.

Thus verses 1-3 are personal praise, while verses 4-7 draw in the whole of mankind. The summary of God's character in verses 8, 9 is almost a repetition of Exodus 34:6, 7 and, in part, Psalm 103:8, 9. The next paragraph (10-13) tells of God's rule, not yet visible to all, but glorious in heaven and earth for those with eyes to see (Isa. 6:3).

The Lord is not only dazzling in glory, but he comes down to human level to meet the needs of the weak (13, 14), and he is the supplier of every creature's needs (15, 16). Today we might say that the instincts or urges for survival in man and the rest of the animal world are indeed a feature of God's creative plan. Where these urges cannot be properly satisfied, we who have sufficient should fulfil God's plan by helping to supply what others lack.

Finally, we are not to sit down passively and wait, but we must keep the lines open between God and ourselves (17-19) and thus be drawn out in love for him (20). A casual reader might think it a pity to 'spoil' a beautiful psalm with the destruction of the wicked (20), but the psalms are realistic, and judgement is certain. Even a psalm of praise carries a warning. (Note also the ending of Psalm 139.)

THOUGHT: How has the reality of God, as David sees it, come home to me lately?

146 Grounds for praise

The remainder of the psalms, all anonymous, begin and end with Hallelujah (see note on Ps. 111). Some of the themes of Psalm 145:14-20 are taken up and amplified, all extolling the character of God as worthy of praise.

Man has a limited time on earth to show forth the glory of God. The psalmist, who might still be David in view of the sentiments repeated from Psalm 145, wants his life to be filled with praise (1, 2). Even so, life on earth is short, and no man, not even a prince, can secure eternal existence on earth for himself or others (3, 4; 49:7-9 margin).

Even God does not give exemption from death, but those who have put their confidence in him (5) may be sure that he will never lose his hold of them, since his promises are for ever, and he is the Creator and Upholder of all (6; 17:15; 49:15; 73:25-28).

As in the story of the Pharisee and the tax-collector (Luke 18:9-14), the Lord listens to those who know their need (7-9), and Jesus pointed out that it is the sick who need to call the doctor (Matt. 9:12, 13). So the psalmist speaks of the oppressed, including, today, prisoners of conscience and those deprived of human rights.

The repetition of the Lord (Jehovah) at the beginning of every line in verses 7b-9 is a glorious affirmation that it is the God who revealed himself in covenant with Israel who cares for those whom man often disregards or ill-treats (Jer. 7:6). Yet here we find him also concerned for the non-Israelite sojourner (9), who attaches himself to a family or to the community. There may have been more of these than we realise, since they are taken for granted in the Ten Commandments (Exod. 20:10; also Lev. 16:29; 25:35, 47; Num. 35:15). Obviously, if they stayed for any length of time, they would accept the Jewish faith (Num. 15:14-16; 19:10), and ultimately their descendants would be absorbed into Israel. The word used in Psalm 146:9 was used later of proselytes, i.e. Gentile converts to Judaism.

THOUGHT: Set this psalm alongside the hymn,
'Fill Thou my life, O Lord my God,
In every part with praise . . . .'

147 God, nature and man

This is one of the few psalms with anything much to say about God and nature (see also 8, 29, 104, 148). God is seen as the Creator and Upholder of all things, but especially as the one who has made himself known to Israel. The two thoughts are intermingled.

Thus verses 1-3 celebrate the return from exile and the rebuilding of Jerusalem by Nehemiah. This is set against the background of God's gracious care for the broken-hearted and downtrodden, as the Jews had been in Babylon. But God is not only the God who moves in history. His power is seen in the stars, each one of which has its place in his plan and purpose (4; Isa. 40:26). His care is seen on earth, where the seasons of his year bring the growth of food for animals and for birds (8, 9).

Yet God's greatest pleasure is not in the powerful war horse (10; Job 39:19-25), nor in the speed of a swift runner (10). Ultimately his joy is to build up a firm relationship with mankind (11).

The psalm returns to its beginning, with praise for the newly rebuilt city with its strong gates (13; Neh. 3.3, 6). There had been harvest problems soon after the return when the people neglected the rebuilding of the Temple (Hag. 1:9-11), but now there was prosperity (14). There had been powerful attempts to thwart Nehemiah (Neh. 4), but now there was peace (14; Neh. 6:16).

Then there is a return to God's control of nature. He is the commander, whose word must be obeyed (15; Isa. 55:10, 11). It is curious that the psalmist dwells on the cold winter (16-18), since snow and ice are not normal features of Judea, although they are familiar in the north. Perhaps recent blizzards had impressed the writer because he had not seen them before. For other rare references see 2 Samuel 23:20; Job 37:6; 38:22; Proverbs 31:21. The comparisons that follow are of a type that would occur to one who was not familiar with snow, hail, and frost. The various translations are interesting: 'Snow like a blanket' (GNB, JB). The 'ice' is clearly hail. Thus 'hail like pebbles' (NIV), 'hail like gravel' (GNB), 'hail like breadcrumbs' (NEB, JB).

God's power in creation gives place to his revelation in Scripture (19, 20), since nature by itself shows no more than the fact of a Creator with 'eternal power and deity' (Rom. 1:20). God's way, both in Old and New Testament times, is to reveal himself to a small nucleus of people who will then become his witnesses to the world.

THOUGHT: How far does this psalm bring together God in nature and God in the believer's life?

148 Total praise

The contents of this psalm cover the whole universe, visible and invisible; but once more it has its climax in covenant redemption and revelation. Invisible to us is the host of angels (1, 2). Although some fell with Satan (2 Pet. 2:4) there is a vast multitude around the throne of God of those who constantly reflect his praise (Rev. 5:11, 12) and fulfil his commissions (103:20; Heb. 1:14).

One can understand how personal beings can praise God, but it would not easily occur to us that inanimate things could also praise him (3, 4). Yet the Bible is sure that they can, and we see that their praise lies in fulfilling perfectly the purpose for which they were made. In this way they tell out the glory of God, just as a beautiful machine commends its maker (19:1-4). We may say that the dependable orderliness of all creation speaks of the mind of the Creator, and indeed makes possible the physical sciences (6).

From angels we descend to the sun, moon, and stars, and from them to the unlimited (highest) heavens, and to the clouds that float high up in the upper air (3, 4). The psalmist probably has Genesis 1 in mind, where God separates the clouds from the waters on earth, with the firmament, or expanse, between (Gen. 1:6, 7). This expanse is described in verse 20 as 'the firmament of the heavens', where birds fly and clouds float. We have applied verses 5 and 6 to the whole creation as well as to the heavenly bodies.

The depths and their inhabitants counterbalance the heights (7), so that all are subservient to God, as also are the elements (8), the earth's crust, and the vegetation that provides food and shelter (9, 10). As in Genesis 1, man is the climax; so the psalm calls on all human beings to fulfil the purpose of their creation, and thus join in the praise of Jehovah (11, 12). For he is the only God, and is infinitely greater than the universe he has created (13). Moreover, he has given special strength to the people of Israel, and taken them into covenant relationship (14).

THOUGHT: Read the hymn, 'All creatures of our God and King' alongside of this psalm.

149 Response in praise

This psalm speaks of two ways of praising God. The first (1-6a) raises few problems. Believers who gather together for worship gather to join in praise, and continually find a freshness in God's ways with them (1; 33:3; 96:1, 2). They praise God joyfully for their creation and for preservation under his rule (2).

Praise can be expressed in physical ways, particularly in music, which has always been prominent in times of Christian revival, and also in dancing. This has been generally omitted in Christian worship, probably because of pagan and sexual connotations, but has been revived today by some Christian groups (3).

To know the Lord's favour is a very happy experience (4; Luke 10:20; 1 Pet. 1:3-6), but it is also very humbling, since it is 'not because of works' (4; Eph. 2:8-10). With sins forgiven, and clear consciences, the faithful praise God both day and night (5; 4:4; 17:3; 42:8).

One could wish that the second part of the psalm (6-9), with its zeal for God's victory expressed with such ferocity, had not been written, but it stands as part of the word of God. Certainly the psalmist wishes to join in the ultimate victory of God, and for this we commend his zeal. But his methods of carrying out God's purposes are far removed from the Sermon on the Mount, although sadly they would be well understood under some modern dictatorships.

Let us suppose that God took the psalmist aside. 'You want to see me recognised as Lord of the world and to share my victory. One day I shall call the world to judgement, and when I pronounce sentence you will see it through my eyes and approve. Meanwhile I will show you a deeper fulfilment of your words than you can realise at present. It certainly concerns life and death. My Son will come, and he will commission my followers to a new battle for the lives of great and small. His death will be as horrible as the deaths that you foresee in your psalm, because he will give his life in exchange for the lives of the people that you see as doomed to death. Would it not be wonderful if they, like you, could become my faithful ones (9), and, after receiving his death as their own (Rom. 6:5-8; Col. 2:13, 14), pass from death to life?'

This is only a suggestion for interpreting a difficult passage. We must remember that there will certainly be death sentences at the judgement day, and that meanwhile the spread of the gospel can be expressed in terms of battle and conquest (e.g. 1 Cor. 9:26, 27; 15:57; 2 Cor. 10:3; Eph. 6:10-18; 1 Tim. 1:18; 6:12; 2 Tim. 2:4; 4:7; Rev. 6:2; 12:7; 17:14).

THOUGHT: Which is better, to have the zeal of the psalmist or to atrophy with indifference?

150 All praise

This is a fine outgoing psalm with which to round off the book. We have met a great deal of introspection, and the Christian life needs this, as long as it is not morbid. But praise asks nothing for ourselves, yet gives us new vitality.

Commentators differ over whether God's sanctuary (1) is earthly or heavenly, but the JB has a neat rendering, 'Praise God in his Temple on earth, praise him in his temple in heaven'. So we join the angels in their praises, praising God both for his deeds and for what he is in himself (2). Praise is emotional, and normally we need not be afraid of stirring our emotions with music (3-5). There is poor music, but equally there is fine and uplifting music, not only in hymns, that makes us glad that God has given us such a gift.

All living creatures praise him by being what they are, and thus fulfilling the purpose for which God made them (6). Occasionally verse 6 is inscribed above a church organ, and why not?

A few concluding thoughts on the whole book of Psalms will not be out of place. The psalms show how men of God respond to God under various circumstances. They face inner and outer enemies. They are puzzled by God's apparent inactivity when history shows how he has intervened in the past. Though they cannot see beyond this life they break through to God in faith. They know the security of belonging to God, and they are jealous for his honour when attacks on themselves and the chosen people come from those who spurn his standards. At times they are given prophetic glimpses of the coming Messiah and his rule after his sufferings. But they live before God's final revelation in Christ, and we must always see how the true principles of godliness are remoulded in the New Testament.

THOUGHT: 'True praise is not abstract but issues from experience' (H. L. Ellison).

Questions for further study and discussion on Psalms 142–150

1. On a piece of paper write a list under the heading, 'I am good at' (compare notes on Psalms 144). If you are in a group, let each member of the group do a list for one other member. Compare your list and that written about you. What do you learn from this? Praise God for your abilities, and those of your Christian friends.

2. Are you doing the work God wants you to do? How can you know? (Compare Psa. 138:8, and the comment on Psa. 148: 'Praise lies in fulfilling perfectly the purpose for which they were made.')

3. Do you believe that war is ever necessary for a Christian?

4. Have the last six psalms of the Psalter taught you anything about praise and worship? Have they suggested any ways in which the worship of your own community might perhaps be improved?

5. The immigrant to our country is the modern equivalent of the sojourner in Psalm 146:9. In what ways does your church, and you yourself, seek to care for the immigrants in your area? Can anything more be done?

6. In what ways can we praise God in our everyday lives?

7. Summarise what you have learnt from your study of the Psalter.

8. Suggest ways in which you should change your life as a result of your study.